Praise for *The Entrepreneur* (1st edition)

"*The Entrepreneur* is a must-read for managers and those who want to be their own boss. The 21 rules are indeed a set of golden rules, distilled from real experiences...All in all, don't miss it."

Bangkok Post

"It is rare to get a business book that is both entertaining and useful. Michael Bloomberg's *Bloomberg on Bloomberg* was one. Bill Heinecke has written another. It is simple and easy to read and understand his 21 rules... The great virtue is that he is honest enough to admit his failures and has a sense of humor about his shortcomings."

Hong Kong Standard

"The fact that this book relates the remarkable life story of William Heinecke alone justifies it as being an extremely enjoyable and informative read... It has a very easy-to-read formula, crisp writing and loads of street-wise advice."

New Straits Times

"In *The Entrepreneur*, Heinecke draws on his own experiences to highlight some of the crucial dos and don'ts of making a go of it in business. And he's not afraid to use his own past slip-ups to illustrate some of the 'don'ts'. This is probably the biggest selling point of *The Entrepreneur*. Its personal touch makes for a highly entertaining read..."

Asian Business

"Heinecke's autobiography is a good read... I was reminded of Richard Branson's autobiography. Both books offer an insight into the personality of the entrepreneur, and both are good because their writers are even more enlightening about their business failures than their successes."

Finance Asia

THE ENTREPRENEUR

Twenty-Five Golden Rules
For The Global Business Manager

Revised Edition

THE ENTREPRENEUR

Twenty-Five Golden Rules
For The Global Business Manager

Revised Edition

William Heinecke
with
Jonathan Marsh

John Wiley & Sons (Asia) Pte Ltd

Other Wiley Editorial Offices

John Wiley & Sons, Inc., 111 River Street, Hoboken, NJ 07030, USA
John Wiley & Sons Ltd, The Atrium, Southern Gate, Chichester PO19 8SQ, England
John Wiley & Sons (Canada) Ltd, 22 Worcester Road, Rexdale, Ontario M9W 1L1, Canada
John Wiley & Sons Australia Ltd, 33 Park Road (PO Box 1226), Milton, Queensland 4064, Australia
Wiley-VCH, Pappelallee 3, 69469 Weinheim, Germany

Library of Congress Catalogning-in- Publication Data
978-0-470-82098-8

Typeset in 11/17 points, Stone Serif by Linographic Services Pte Ltd

10

To my wife Kathy, and children John and David, who have been my greatest inspiration, as well as my mother Connie, my brother Skip and the over 10,000 associates whose support has made the Minor Group the success we are today.

Contents

Preface

Do you think you have what it takes to be an entrepreneur?

An entrepreneur is a person who gauges the risks and rewards of a business and works quickly to initiate, organize, and manage a particular opportunity, idea, or concept. The key words are "risk" and "business." The entrepreneur will often risk more, work harder, and demand more of himself or herself than any ordinary business person. The rewards, however, can be immeasurable.

Intrigued? If so, then perhaps the time has come to be your own boss. But before you quit your nice, cushy job with the monthly pay check, the modern office, the efficient secretary, and that comfortable feeling of security that comes with working for an established organization, consider the guidelines for success presented in this book. Bill Heinecke has spent a lifetime doing business in a challenging, ever-changing environment. These "rules" should help anyone who wants to follow in his footsteps.

Introduction

In 1967, an American teenager with a high school education, a blank résumé, and slender financial resources strode into a lawyer's office in Bangkok. He handed over the equivalent of US$1,000 and signed the necessary papers to register two companies, Inter-Asian Enterprise and Inter-Asian Publicity. While the names sounded grand, their assets were meager. The registration fee gobbled up most of the US$1,200 the young man had borrowed from a moneylender; what little remained was spent on plastic buckets and floor mops for his new cleaning business, and a few minutes of air time on a local radio station. Cleaning offices and writing simple advertisements wasn't glamorous work, but it was a start. Bill Heinecke had taken his first faltering step into the world of commerce.

Thirty-five years later, that teenager has turned 53 and sits on top of a sprawling business empire. He has become the most successful foreign businessman in Thailand and perhaps one of the smartest expatriate entrepreneurs in the whole of Southeast Asia. Heinecke has persuaded the spice-loving Thais to eat pizza; he has built luxury hotels and shopping malls where others feared to tread; he has spotted trends and opportunities where competitors saw only red ink and dead ends. Scattered over the country is a chain of more than a hundred pizza restaurants, two ice cream franchises, steak restaurants, and a host of manufacturing and licensing operations that include the world's largest golf glove factory, Esprit fashion, Sheaffer pens, cosmetics, and a company that provides catering to offshore oil rigs. He is the chief executive and major shareholder of three publicly listed companies —

The Minor Food Group, Royal Garden Resorts and the Minor Corporation — that employ more than 12,000 people. In 1998, *AsiaMoney* magazine voted Heinecke's The Pizza plc one of Thailand's best-managed companies. A few months later, *Forbes* named it one of the best 300 small companies in the world — it was the only Thai company to be nominated.

Heinecke is well respected by the business community in Thailand. Chanita Panpruet, head of debt restructuring at ING Baring, Thailand, describes him as "a pioneer." "He started the concept of Western fast-food chains in Thailand and made it a success. Many people said it wouldn't work. 'Pizza in Thailand?' they said. 'He must be crazy!' But he got the timing right. Thais were willing to try Western ideas, and he spotted that. His timing was immaculate. He has also shown an ability to cope with adversity, to survive difficult times. He is one of a handful of people who have always run a transparent business. He has always been very upfront. Everyone is going to have to follow his lead now. Times have changed."

Korn Chatikavanij, the president of JP Morgan Securities (Thailand), echoes those sentiments. "He is unique — a foreigner who has become totally assimilated into the Thai business world. He moves from Amcham [the American Chamber of Commerce] to a Thai business environment quite effortlessly. What stands out about him is that he is very aggressive but also fair. You know what you're dealing with. He's a real professional, and he knows a good deal when he sees one. He was the trendsetter in corporate transparency. He backs entrepreneurial skills with great management."

These days the mop and bucket business have disappeared. Heinecke flies himself around Thailand in a Piper Malibu, and after a long day in the office returns home by limousine to a beautiful house he shares with Kathy, his wife of more than 30 years, and Ben, a huge Great Dane. When Heinecke built the house 15 years ago, it was surrounded by rice paddies. Now, reflecting the changes that have taken place in Bangkok, the house is just out of sight and earshot of a teeming highway. Like Bangkok, his adopted home, Heinecke has had to overcome a great many challenges to get where he is today.

Indeed, on July 2, 1997, it appeared that what had taken 30 years to build was in danger of collapsing. That was the day the Asian financial crisis hit. The baht plummeted, interest rates soared, empires crashed, and vast fortunes were lost. In January 1998, the man whom *Forbes* had estimated as being worth US$100 million reckoned the figure was closer to zero.

Some thought that Heinecke had started to take his foot off the pedal before the crash, but he was back in the driving seat the moment it happened.

He took the unprecedented step of calling a meeting of all the executives from all three of his publicly companies and told them straight out: "We're in trouble." One of the senior executives said later: "It was the sign of a great leader. He could see there was a battle coming and that half the troops didn't even know there was a war on. The other half were ready to fight but didn't quite know what to do. He showed them and led from the front." Heinecke's empire not only survived Asia's worst recession in living memory, but the 1998 annual reports were full of positive news about record revenues and profits.

His troubles were not over. He became embroiled in a gruelling battle with a U.S. corporate giant over the same pizza franchise for Thailand that had helped to make him so successful. He emerged victorious by launching his own pizza brand. Then came the September 11 terrorist attacks in the United States and the commercial aftershocks that rippled through industries linked to travel and tourism. Again, he survived by thinking quickly and taking decisive action.

So, what is Heinecke's secret? How did a high school kid with no professional qualifications become a millionaire by the time he was 21 in a country where he could hardly speak the language? It is a fascinating story. In 1967, when Heinecke set out on his entrepreneurial journey with mop and bucket in hand, it was a time of political unrest and turmoil in the region:

- Thailand had agreed to allow the U.S. government to launch B-52 bombing raids on Vietnam from its airbases, and a Thai contingent of 2200 soldiers arrived in Saigon (now Ho Chi Minh City) to fight alongside the South Vietnamese.
- In the United States, public opposition to the Vietnam War was growing. President Lyndon Johnson announced that the American military would stop bombing North Vietnam in exchange for "productive discussions."
- Martial law was declared in five northern Thai provinces following increased communist activity.
- Red Guards were on the rampage as the Cultural Revolution devastated China.
- The Association of Southeast Asian Nations (ASEAN) was founded by Indonesia, Malaysia, Thailand, Singapore, and the Philippines at a conference in Bangkok. ASEAN's main objective was to promote economic development through regional cooperation.
- General Suharto took power in Indonesia, replacing President Sukarno.
- The Singapore dollar was issued as the new currency of the island state.
- The last British troops left Malaysia.

They were unstable times, but politics didn't concern the young Heinecke. He had more important things on his mind — like survival. Having turned down the chance to study at a prestigious university in the United States, he was under great pressure to prove to his parents that he was capable of standing on his own two feet. What he lacked in experience, he made up for in enthusiasm. He possessed a sharp eye for spotting opportunities, an insatiable appetite for hard work, and an uncanny ability to combine business with pleasure.

Heinecke was passionate about motor racing, whether it be in go-karts, motorcycles, or cars. Within months of going into business, he persuaded Ford to sponsor him in an outrageous attempt to set an overland driving record between Singapore and Bangkok. The challenge was to complete the 900-mile (1450-kilometer) journey in less than 30 hours, an almost impossible target given the state of the roads at that time. There were also other minor considerations, such as communist rebels on the Thai–Malaysian border, monsoon rains, and barely fordable rivers, not to mention the likelihood of bumping into an elephant or two. All in all, it was quite a challenge for a novice driver in a Ford Cortina.

The deal was a simple one: if he succeeded, he would pick up all the sponsorship money; if he failed, he would have to cover the expenses himself. It was a huge gamble, as failure would have just about wiped him out. To attract additional publicity, Heinecke talked a friend into joining him. His choice was a sound one: his co-driver was Albert Poon, a renowned racing driver from Hong Kong. After the pair crossed the causeway from Singapore, they made splendid progress through Malaysia and were on schedule as they approached the Thai border. Then disaster struck. Poon did not have the correct visa for Thailand, and no amount of pleading would change the minds of the immigration authorities. Two precious hours were wasted on the fruitless negotiations before the decision was made for Heinecke to go to Thailand alone.

The roads on the Thai side of the border were much harder going, but, with his foot to the floor, Heinecke drove non-stop through the night toward Bangkok. Amazingly, he made it in one piece, completing the journey with just one hour and 20 minutes to spare. The story of his remarkable drive was widely reported in the press, and Heinecke became a star. The sponsorship money went straight into his fledgling businesses.

He soon followed this triumph with another, driving a Honda S6000 from the Laotian capital of Vientiane to Bangkok in six hours. His companies were now growing at the same speed as Heinecke's reputation as a racing driver — fast.

The following year, 1968, he found time to marry Kathy, his high school sweetheart. They honeymooned first in Thailand and then in Hong Kong, where they stayed at the luxurious Mandarin Hotel. Heinecke was now making some money and bought himself an E-Type Jaguar to mark the occasion of his marriage.

Success followed him everywhere. The advertising and office cleaning businesses continued to prosper, and Heinecke competed with great success at the Macau Grand Prix, then Asia's premier motor sport event. In 1970, he started exploring other business opportunities and set up the Minor Corporation, a company that he still controls today. Life was good. And then it got better. In the early 1970s, Ogilvy & Mather, one of the world's leading advertising agencies, started expanding in Asia. They opened an office in Thailand, but found the going tough and were soon looking around for someone who knew the market. It wasn't long before they realized Heinecke was the man they needed.

Michael Ball, a senior Ogilvy executive who later founded the Ball Partnership advertising agency, took the decision to hire him and still remembers those days fondly. Ball identified five qualities in Heinecke: ambition, a sharp mind that got straight to the heart of an issue, a desire to learn, persistence, and a complete lack of fear.

> *He was so ambitious. If we had been in the United States, he would certainly be running for company president. He managed to build an agency with great local talent without really knowing anything about advertising. He was good at getting clients, but he didn't have much idea of what to do with them after that except to hand them over to the people who did. His view is that he can pick up the necessary knowledge later, or hire someone who has it. Bill didn't want to sell his advertising agency but Ogilvy wanted 100% ownership. He haggled like hell and, boy, does he drive a hard bargain!*
>
> *But it gave him the opportunity to learn about advertising for the first time. David Ogilvy was the great advertising guru. He was the first person who tried to codify advertising by writing down hundreds of guidelines. He called them 'Magic Lanterns.' Bill was very impressed — he has a great hunger for knowledge — and he could quote them word for word.*
>
> *This was the most formative period of his life. He really learnt about advertising and realized that with knowledge comes power. Ogilvy led the way in codifying, measuring, benchmarking, call it what you like — but it was a way of forming a body of knowledge, rules,*

guidelines, and principles. This opened Bill's eyes to the potential of a lot of other businesses. The agency was a huge success, but we had hundreds of fights.

One time, we were in Bangkok arguing over a salary increase. Bill's claim wasn't on the small side and, if granted, would have set a precedent for the whole region. A secretary burst in and said there was going to be a coup, a regular occurrence in those days, and everyone should go home. The announcement coincided with a torrential rainstorm. I had to leave to fly to London, but Bill jumped in the car and chewed my ear all the way to the airport. It was crazy — the whole town was in a panic, the roads were flooding, the traffic was a mess, and the airconditioning had broken down — but that didn't stop Bill from trying to convince me he was right.

He just has no fear. Once he's convinced that he wants to do something, it's very hard to stop him. He has a sharp mind that gets to the core issue. He has a foot-to-the-floor style and is incredibly persistent. And, yes, we're still good friends!

Anil Thadani, the doyen of Asian direct investment who is now chairman of Schroder Capital Partners (Asia), has known Heinecke for 20 years.

I first met Bill in the early 1980s. I had recently formed what was then Asia's first private equity/venture capital business with a couple of partners, and one of my partners had met Heinecke on a visit to Bangkok. When he returned to Hong Kong, he told me about Bill and said that I should meet with him because he was the kind of person who could turn out to be a good partner for us in Thailand.

I met Bill a few weeks later when he was visiting Hong Kong. He described his business to me and it was clear from that meeting that this was a consummate entrepreneur with no real business plan of where he was going. He had a mishmash of businesses consisting of agencies distributing an unlikely mix of western consumer products, from cosmetics to engineering components! He came off as a deal junkie who could not say no to any deal that was brought to him. He had even ventured into the food business with a Mister Donut franchise! As disorganized as he seemed in his business, there was something intuitively attractive about him — I guess you can call it star quality — the look of a man who is going to make it.

At the time we met, he was looking to raise a very modest amount of money to rationalize his financial affairs and keep some of his bankers happy. I must say, I took an instant liking to him and we decided to make the investment. Unlike some other Asian entrepreneurs that we have invested with, we found Bill very cooperative, consultative and fair in all his dealings with us. He asked me to go on the board of all of his companies and I have been a director of his group of companies ever since.

William E. Heinecke was born in a U.S. naval hospital in Virginia, in the United States, in 1949. The following year, just as the Korean War broke out, the family, which included Bill's older brother, Skip, moved to California. Bill's father, Roy, was soon sent to Tokyo to work for *Leatherneck* magazine, the journal of the U.S. Marine Corps. His mother, Connie, determined not to be left behind in California with the children while her husband enjoyed himself in Asia, decided to follow. Without telling Roy, she booked tickets on a tramp steamer that was taking fish oil to Japan and, four weeks later, she and the two boys arrived in the Japanese port of Sasebo. She had US$60 in her pocket. She then broke the news of his family's arrival to her husband in Tokyo. After a 28-hour train journey in a third-class compartment, Connie, Skip, and Bill reached Tokyo covered in soot. Three baths later, they were clean and ready to explore the first of their many homes in Asia.

After two years in Japan, Roy retired from the Marines and the family returned to the United States. However, they didn't settle and in 1956 they came East again, this time to Hong Kong, where Roy worked for the United States Information Services in the U.S. Consulate in Hong Kong.

Bill has lived in Asia ever since. In 1960, the Heineckes moved to Kuala Lumpur and then to Bangkok in 1963.

Bill's entrepreneurial flair comes from his mother. Connie's grandfather was a captain in the German Navy who moved to New York in 1912, where he opened one of the early cinema schools. Another relative became the head of Paramount Studios in California. Her father was an inventor who had a broad range of interests and traveled widely, but rarely had a regular pay check or a settled home. As a child, Connie sold newspapers, magazines, and candy in Philadelphia during the Depression. "I knew what life was all about from a pretty early age," she said. "It was survival of the fittest. If you didn't go out there and hustle, you didn't eat. It was as simple as that. My attitude to any job has always been, just do it. All they can do is fire you."

Bill's father, a Marine who had fought in World War II, was a man of books at heart. Roy never did anything impulsively, but Connie made up for it. When the family lived in Japan, she became women's editor of *Army Times*. During the war, she traveled with Marilyn Monroe all over Korea holding the honorary rank of colonel, which made her senior to her husband. Within months of moving to Hong Kong, Connie joined a small agency called Cathay Advertising and was soon selling ad space for *Newsweek*. Before long, she was making more money than her husband.

In Kuala Lumpur, at the age of ten, Bill started helping out at a cafe run by an old couple who had befriended him. He was soon giving them advice about how they could improve the business by changing their marketing and advertising strategy. "He seemed to be born with an old head on his young shoulders," said Connie. "He always took charge of everything. I sent him to a nursery school in California and he started a lemonade stand. 'How much are you going to charge?' I asked him. 'Twenty-five cents,' came the reply, and a quarter was worth something in those days. 'If I charge two cents, I'm going to have to stand in the hot sun all day. But if I charge 25 cents, I can sell three glasses and retire.'"

In 1963, Thailand beckoned, and Bill attended the International School of Bangkok. It wasn't long, though, before he found another outlet for his entrepreneurial bent. As a 14-year-old, he helped to introduce the sport of go-karting to the country. As interest in the pastime grew, he suggested writing a column for the *Bangkok World*, a newspaper that was later taken over by the *Bangkok Post*. The editor agreed to pay for the column on the condition that Bill secured advertisements to run alongside. All the go-kart suppliers were keen to oblige, and Bill's column became a regular feature. Soon he was also writing advertising supplements about motor cars — there were a lot of them about in Bangkok, even in those days. Then one day the advertising manager quit. As Bill had been acting as his unofficial deputy, he soon found himself in the office every day selling advertising space.

At 17, Bill knew what it felt like to have a regular income and money in his pocket. It felt good. He could afford to buy a motorcycle, and to move on to faster go-karts as the sport grew. At 18, to his parents' horror, he made the decision that changed his life — he turned down the chance to go to college in the U.S., borrowed US$1,200, and walked into a lawyer's office to register his first two companies.

There is no doubt that it was his experiences at Ogilvy & Mather, when he was in his twenties, that broadened Heinecke's horizons and shaped his future as an entrepreneur. After a few years as an O&M employee, he began to feel restless. At first, he had enjoyed working for someone else and not having to shoulder all the responsibility for a business. But after a couple of years it became too comfortable and he decided he wanted to be his own boss again. All the skills he had picked up during his time with the agency soon paid off, as he moved into a whole range of new businesses — import, export, manufacturing, hotels and, eventually, fast food.

Never one to stand still, Heinecke also found another challenge — flying. He took lessons in Thailand and then went to the United States to get his pilot's license. He realized that, with his own plane, he would be able to combine business with pleasure. With a burgeoning empire, what better way was there for an entrepreneur to keep an eye on business? He bought a plane, a Beechcraft, in the United States and had it flown across the Atlantic to London. The pilot, a German woman by the name of Margrit Waltz, flew for TNA Aviation. "Tits 'n Ass Aviation — all women pilots," she explained. Ambitious as ever, Heinecke wanted to fly the plane on to Bangkok himself. Waltz was an accomplished pilot and they completed the grueling journey in just four days. Heinecke, who became one of the first pilots to fly into Burma since World War II, can be seen most weekends lining up in his Piper Malibu behind jumbo jets at Bangkok's Don Muang Airport waiting to take off for Chiang Mai, Hua Hin, Pattaya, or Phuket.

Heinecke's businesses continued to bloom. In 1980, the first Pizza Hut opened in Pattaya, followed four years later by his first luxury hotel in Hua Hin. In 1986, he moved into the luxury ice cream market, and then, in 1989, he opened the world's largest golf glove factory. More luxury hotels followed, a joint venture was formed with fashion chain Esprit, and Pizza Huts sprouted up all over the country. In 1995, Heinecke's pride and joy, the six-star Regent Chiang Mai, opened to rave reviews.

But it hasn't all been success and good news. In 1994, he lost a close friend and business associate, Suwit Wanglee, in a flying accident. A senior member of the Wanglee banking family, (Mr) Khun Suwit was chairman of the Marriott Royal Garden Riverside Hotel and one of the most prominent businessmen in the country. The death of his friend taught Bill Heinecke a bitter lesson about the importance of communication.

Khun Suwit suffered from high blood pressure and always took the precaution of taking another experienced pilot along with him when he flew. On this occasion, it was a communication problem in the cockpit, not Khun Suwit's health, that proved fatal. The co-pilot assumed that he would only be called into action if his boss fell ill. Khun Suwit, meanwhile, assumed that as his co-pilot was a far more experienced pilot, he would speak up if he detected a problem. Everything conspired against Khun Suwit that day. He was in a hurry to get to a meeting in Phrae, in northern Thailand. They were descending in bad weather and, as the airport's weather radar was broken, he was unaware that they were flying too low. The co-pilot, who had flown into the airport many times, would have been aware of this but apparently failed to speak up. In Thailand, for a junior to speak before spoken to by a senior would be considered as bad manners. They hit the very top of a mountain. Another 50 metres and they would have lived.

When the news broke that Khun Suwit's plane was missing, Heinecke realized that Thailand didn't subscribe to the worldwide emergency satellite system that could pick up signals from a downed plane. Although he had been a Thai citizen since 1991, Heinecke called in a favor and rang the American ambassador, who immediately alerted the Federal Aviation Administration (FAA) in Washington.

The FAA was picking up signals from northern Thailand and gave Heinecke the coordinates. He passed them on to the authorities and then flew his own plane north with Khun Suwit's brother, Khun Suchin and his wife, Pia, to join the search. The old military maps were very basic and the terrain was rugged, but Heinecke had a portable Global Positioning System which helped to pinpoint the crash site. They found the wreckage the next day. Neither man had stood a chance, as the plane had hit a solid wall of rock at 180 mph. It was a heartbreaking sight for Heinecke, who had encouraged his friend to take up flying.

Professionally, Heinecke is the first to admit that not everything he has touched has turned to gold. Far from it. There have been some expensive flops and setbacks. The occasional failure has taught him that you cannot win all the time. Another skill he has learnt is how to box cleverly when climbing into the ring with an opponent who packs a bigger punch. The most recent example was in 1999, when there was an opportunity to take a controlling interest in the Regent Bangkok, widely regarded as one of the best business hotels in the world. A block of shares was put up for sale and Heinecke's Royal Garden Resort company, which already owned 25% of the Regent, saw this as the chance of a lifetime. It was not to be. Goldman Sachs, the powerful U.S. investment bank, made a bid Heinecke couldn't match. But all was not lost. By making some smart tactical plays and using his local knowledge, he stopped Goldman Sachs from taking control of a hotel for which he felt genuine affection.

The Asian crisis proved he could recover from loss and disappointment quickly. And the next big project? "Deals are like buses," he says. "There will always be another one along in a while."

Spoken like a true entrepreneur.

Rule

1

Find A Vacuum and Fill It

Small opportunities are often the beginning of great enterprises.
— Demosthenes

There is one thing stronger than all the world and that is an idea whose time has come. **— Victor Hugo**

S o, you think you have what it takes to be an entrepreneur. You have read all those success stories about other people making it big and it is making you restless. You are good at your job, and people at work keep saying you have a great future, but you are tired of taking mediocre orders from mediocre people. And why is it that you are the one with all the bright ideas, yet someone else always gets the credit? When is that big promotion coming — the one with the serious money, share options and the mega bonus? "In a while," they keep saying, "in a while." The time has come to be your own boss. But first, some words of warning before you quit your nice, comfortable job with the monthly pay check, the modern office, the efficient secretary, and that warm feeling of security that comes with working for an established organization.

Your boss, colleagues, and many of your friends are going to think you have lost your mind. Expect one or all of the following remarks. "Are you crazy?" ... "You are ruining a promising career" ... "In five years' time you could be regional manager/ senior partner in New York/head of the Hong Kong office/the managing director in Singapore" (delete as applicable).

It takes a lot of courage to sign that letter of resignation. So, before you take that great leap into the unknown, I suggest that you sit down and ponder the following issues raised in an article by Brian O'Reilly, published in *Fortune* magazine, entitled "What it Takes to Start a Startup." O'Reilly really gets to the heart of the matter.

Getting the entrepreneurial bug, are you? Tired of reading about all those pubescent little CEOs who did nothing more clever than sell books or airline tickets over the Internet and made a billion? Meanwhile you, despite your

15 years at that same desk job, have been nursing this fabulous idea. There's just one problem: Every time you think about purchasing that dream, your palms sweat. No steady pay check. No time for golf. How, you wonder, do these entrepreneurs summon the brass ones to risk everything — income, lifestyle, self esteem — on one crazy idea that probably won't work anyway. Better hunker down at that day job. Entrepreneurially speaking, you ain't going nowhere. Are they thrill-seeking lunatics? Despite their image, entrepreneurs are not the Evel Knievels of the business world. Nor do they think much about risk, sweaty palms, wealth power, or failure. If you are terrified at the prospect of becoming an entrepreneur, or are busy dreaming of the power that success will bring, you're probably not cut out for this line of work.[1]

O'Reilly then went on to quote British billionaire Richard Branson, the man who started Virgin Records and Virgin Atlantic Airlines but also attracted publicity through his bold attempts to become the first man to circle the world in a hot-air balloon. "Being an adventurer and an entrepreneur are similar," said Branson. "You're willing to go where most people won't dare. It's not about $2 billion or $3 billion. It's about not wasting your life."

Still convinced you have what it takes to be a successful entrepreneur? OK, but what exactly are you going to do? The first rule of entrepreneurship is to train yourself to see vacuums, or gaps in the market, and then to fill them.

Look around you. See that guy on the street with the sewing machine — what service is he providing? See the woman selling barbecued chicken near those cheap guest houses — why did she choose that location? What about that new hotel on the main road — why is it doing such good business? How come that guy who worked in the computer section is doing so well in his own software design business?

There is one simple answer to all these questions: *these businesses exist because there is a need for them.* It doesn't matter if you are dealing in chicken legs, fancy restaurants, or websites, or whether you are talking about a daily turnover of $100 or $10,000. The principle is the same from Bangkok to Silicon Valley: success in business operates on the principle of finding a vacuum and filling it.

Anita Roddick, who set up the hugely successful Body Shop franchise which sells hype-free cosmetics, once said that if something makes you angry, you have uncovered a gap in the market. If there is a need for a product or service, *someone* is going to jump in and meet it. Why shouldn't it be you? If you are the first to offer the public something it wants and cannot get from anyone else, or if you successfully anticipate a future need, you stand a good chance of striking it rich. Until the competition wakes up to the opportunity that it's missing, you'll have the market all to yourself.

History provides many examples of entrepreneurs who became successful by meeting or anticipating the need for new products. Isaac Merritt Singer produced sewing machines suitable for domestic use; Henry Ford used the assembly-line method to produce automobiles that ordinary people could afford; and George Eastman saw the need for a small, portable camera. Others anticipated demographic trends. Julius Rosenwald of Sears Roebuck, for example, saw the potential for mail-order merchandising; William S. Paley of CBS anticipated the popularity of commercial television as home entertainment; and Ray Kroc of McDonald's saw the potential for a fast-food franchise.

Success has also come to those visionaries who saw how to improve existing goods or services, or who had a gimmick that caught the attention of the marketplace. Steve Jobs redesigned computers so they became simple enough for anyone to use, and Apple was born. And Dewitt and Lila Wallace recycled previously published magazine articles in condensed form in the *Reader's Digest*.

Where do ideas such as these come from? There are three main sources of ideas. The first is your job. The work you're already doing can be a potent source of ideas, because this is where your business instincts have been developed. The second potential source is your hobbies or interests outside of work, as this is another area for which you have a natural feel. The third source is what I call "pedestrian observation," or spotting an opportunity through a casual encounter or an incident in your daily life.

Let me give you a few examples:

- The idea to form Diners Club struck Ralph Schneider when he went out to dinner and discovered he had no cash with him.
- Leo Gerstenzang invented Q-tips when he saw his wife using cotton wool wrapped around a toothpick to clean their baby daughter's ears.
- King C. Gillette got the idea for the safety razor when he became annoyed that his razor was dull one morning. He had been looking for a product that people would use and then throw away.

These people will be remembered as great innovators, but there are also tens of thousands of others who are successful entrepreneurs without becoming household names.

Asia is knee-deep in people who have spotted and then filled vacuums. You don't have to be Li Ka-shing — who started off making plastic flowers and now runs Cheung Kong, one of Hong Kong's most powerful conglomerates — to be a successful entrepreneur. Most are small businessmen and women whose names have never appeared in newspapers but who have made a very good living by seeing an opportunity and having the brains and guts to seize it.

While there is no harm in admiring the major league entrepreneurs, don't forget that they too had to start somewhere. Remember the woman stationed near the guest houses who had spotted a market for her barbecued chicken? One day she might be running a chain of restaurants. And the young computer nerd who set up his own business designing websites might be the next software millionaire.

Let me tell you what worked for me. In 1965, I was a teenager living with my parents in Bangkok and attending the local International School. I suppose I was a pretty normal teenager. I wasn't a very good student, as I was more interested in testing myself against more interesting challenges, such as girls and motor sports.

When I was 14 I was passionate about go-karts, because they were the closest thing to a motorcycle I was allowed to drive. I helped to start the first competitions in Bangkok, and soon there were a lot of people competing in organized races. Before long, this hot new sport had quite a following, and I thought it was about time the press paid some attention to it. I approached an English-language newspaper to see if they were interested in paying me to write a weekly column.

The *Bangkok World* (later bought by the *Bangkok Post*) liked the idea, provided I could guarantee some advertisements to be run next to the column. I knew nothing about selling advertising, but I did know everyone who was connected with the sport. The tire companies who supplied the go-kart drivers and the garage owners were all happy to pay a relatively small amount of money for an ad. It hardly seemed like work at all to me. I was writing about something I loved and doing business with people whom I knew and liked. The newspaper was happy because the ads were bringing in plenty of revenue. Before long, I was earning US$500 a month while I was still at school. I can tell you it felt very good to have a regular income, and back in those days $500 was a lot of money.

The column was going well, so I proposed doing what are now called "advertorials" — supplements in newspapers which are paid for by advertisers. These days, advertorials represent substantial amounts of income for newspapers — look at the *South China Morning Post* and the *Bangkok Post* — but in 1967, it was a ground-breaking concept. There was a vacuum and I was filling it. I set to work writing stories about subjects such as the King of Thailand's private collection of motor cars supported by car advertising. Again, it seemed a perfect business formula: I enjoyed the work, the theme attracted plenty of advertising, and my pocket was bulging with banknotes.

By this time I was spending quite a bit of time in the advertising department of the newspaper office and started to answer the telephone when the manager wasn't around. One day the manager quit and I unofficially inherited his job. At the grand old age of 16, I found myself rushing into the office after school, calling clients, selling space, and generally running the show. When people rang in the morning, they were told: "I'm sorry, the ad manager is in school now. Please call after 3.30 p.m."

I left high school at around the time the ownership of the *Bangkok World* changed; my fortunes changed, too. I wanted to be the full-time advertising manager. The new owner took one look at me and said: "Frankly, I can't entrust my newspaper's advertising to a 17-year-old kid fresh out of high school." I quit the paper on the spot.

Selling advertising was now something I knew a thing or two about, so I looked around for an opportunity that would enable me to exploit that knowledge. In Bangkok, English-language radio was emerging as a new form of media, so I bought some radio time — it was very cheap in those days — hired an announcer, and sold some advertising. I made money from day one. I had no choice, as I had no money to lose.

At the same time, I started an office cleaning company. Why? Because there was a vacuum and I wanted to fill it. A lot of major international companies like Pan Am and AIA were moving into Bangkok. At the same time a lot of office blocks were going up, so there was an increasing demand for this simple service.

It was a little terrifying cleaning the outside of a 20-story building — that was the tallest at the time — in a "hand-made" gondola. I couldn't afford to pay for accident insurance, so I just told the cleaners, "If you fall off, you're fired before you hit the ground." We didn't lose anyone.

Meanwhile, the radio business was expanding into a fledgling media brokerage. We bought radio time, sold the space, and gradually started to write the advertisements as well. Little by little, the business evolved into an advertising agency and I was the boss.

Before I had turned 21, I had 200 people working for me who all had one thing in common: they were all older than I was. If it all sounds too easy, let me tell you a bit about Bangkok in the late 1960s and early 1970s. It was the height of the Vietnam War, so Bangkok was full of Americans and the mighty dollar. Thais were becoming more aware of the outside world through contact with Westerners, and travel and education abroad. A Thai middle class was starting to emerge, creating a host of business opportunities. As the economy expanded, Western companies moved into Bangkok to establish an early foothold and be part of the success story. In short, it was a city of opportunity and I was lucky enough to be in the right place at the right time.

My businesses prospered. Both the advertising agency and the office cleaning service grew as the economy flourished, and I eventually sold both for a lot of money. There are two points to note here: small can indeed be beautiful; and one good thing often leads to another. The go-kart column led to the advertorials, which led to the advertising job, which led to the media brokerage, which led to the advertising agency. Something that had started from one good idea snowballed into one business which became another.

The lessons I learnt as a young entrepreneur proved to be very valuable in later years. We saw, and filled, a vacuum for Western-style fast food in Thailand and became the market leader. Along the way we started the first pizza chain, the first home-delivery service using motorbikes to beat the Bangkok traffic, and the first one-telephone-number ordering service, and we introduced the first premium ice cream.

We were one of the first companies to get into fashion at the time the middle class was emerging and developing an appetite for names like Esprit. Lifestyle products also became very successful. The trick was to spot such trends quickly. We had the advantage of being first in almost everything we did. If you are first, you don't necessarily have to be absolutely brilliant; there will be time to develop and fine-tune things as you go along. But the minute that others start competing for your market share, you had better make sure you are the best. The same rules apply to hotels. We opened the Royal Garden Resort, the first truly modern hotel in Hua Hin. The Railway Hotel had dominated the hotel trade there for half a century, but it didn't put in a swimming pool for its guests until the film *The Killing Fields* was made in Thailand in 1984. In Chiang Mai, we built the Regent, the first six-star hotel in the area.

It doesn't matter how big or small your operation is, the principle remains the same: find that vacuum and fill it fast, before someone else does.

Note

[1] Brian O'Reilly, "What it Takes to Start a Startup," *Fortune*, June 7, 1999.

Rule

2

Do Your Homework

Chance favors the prepared mind. — **Louis Pasteur**

Thought and planning before action is the key to accomplishment. — *Anon*

B efore you can expect to come up with that great idea that will make you a success and dazzle everyone with your business acumen, lightning-quick mind, and all-round brilliance, you must first be willing to spend time researching your chosen subject. A winning idea requires preparation, research, and an ability to think laterally. Whether you are just starting out, looking to expand, or already control a number of businesses, the second rule of successful entrepreneurship is: you must do your homework. If you do this background work properly, you'll be ahead of the pack.

Homework can be fun. As I have already mentioned, a lot of ideas come from casual observation. The idea to set up Pizza Hut in Thailand came when I was sitting in a pizza restaurant in Manila in the late 1970s with a group of friends and I was asked what business ideas might work in Thailand.

I replied, "Look around you." We were in a Shakey's restaurant full of Filipinos and Westerners munching away happily on their pizzas. "I'm sure this would work." The idea stuck in my mind, and the longer I thought about it, the more attractive it became. At the time, there were only a couple of places in Bangkok where you could get a pizza, and they weren't very reliable. So there was no competition to speak of.

Pizza Hut had just been taken over by PepsiCo., so I wrote to the company and it agreed to send someone out to see me. I told the representative that I wanted to try the idea out with one restaurant, but that I didn't want to pay a lot of money for it. I already had the franchise for Mister Donut — one of the first foreign food franchises in Thailand — so I was comfortable with the concept. Pizza Hut seemed keen, and we agreed on a fee of only US$5,000 for the rights to Thailand. (A few years later, the Pizza Hut franchise in Beijing cost me US$50,000!)

Our first Pizza Hut was in Pattaya, the beach resort 60 miles (100 kilometers) east of Bangkok. We figured that if the worst came to the worst and Thais didn't go for pizza, there were always the Western tourists and U.S. navy personnel on R&R leave who flocked to the town. The idea was to minimize the risk. I remember that place very well — I had an apartment on the roof of the building and used to sit out and watch the passing crowds. We didn't make a huge profit, but we were intrigued to see that half of the customers were Thai. The next year we opened a second Pizza Hut in Bangkok. And then another and another. Today, there are more than 200 pizza restaurants in Thailand.

As well as being fun, doing your homework can be a real education. For example, when I was researching the project I was told that it would be unwise to start a pizza operation because Thais don't like cheese. No ifs or buts or maybes — Thais simply wouldn't eat pizza. Actually, there was an element of truth to this. Humans produce an enzyme called lipase which helps to break down milk and dairy products. People who drink milk from an early age keep producing the enzyme, but the opposite applies to those who don't eat or drink dairy products regularly. These people often feel sick if they try to eat, say, cheese. While almost everyone in the West is brought up on milk, cheese, and ice cream, that isn't the case in Asia. In Thailand, many older people still avoid eating dairy products.

I introduced pizza at a time when many things were starting to change in Thailand. The middle class was growing quickly, and many Western ideas were being adopted. Young people had more money in their pockets and were seeking greater choices in lifestyle. Eating pizza in an airconditioned, American-style restaurant became a perfect symbol of increasing purchasing power and changing consumer attitudes.

The success of our pizza restaurants proves my next point. Many years of doing my homework have taught me one very important lesson: people are basically the same the world over, or at least much more so than the experts would have us believe. Almost everyone likes to try new things, and especially so in the emerging markets where new influences are impacting on people's lives. The fact that people worldwide have a great deal more in common today than they did 30 years ago is a result of that unstoppable juggernaut called globalization. The world is shrinking, the cultural gaps bridged by the spread of English, advertising, satellite television and MTV, faster and cheaper air travel, and improved tele-communications, including the Internet and e-mail.

Thomas Friedman, in his book *The Lexus and the Olive Tree*, explores the dangers and benefits of globalization. One morning in the city of Doha in Qatar, he was strolling along a seafront lined with palm trees. He was busy observing the local people in native dress going about their daily lives when he suddenly came across a Taco Bell restaurant with a six-metre picture of the Emir of Qatar protruding from its roof.

People all over the world want in on globalization. Those Qataris who were packing into Taco Bell were not coming from some charming pub or neighbourhood bistro full of polished brass and oak. Before Taco Bell there was probably a fly-infested sidewalk stand, some guy grilling on charcoals in less than sanitary conditions, no lighting and no bathroom. In its place Qataris were being offered something they had never tasted before — Mexican food — with a clean bathroom, international sanitation standards, smiling service and quality controls, all at a price they could afford.

And there is something more they were being offered. I discovered it in Malaysia. I was introduced to a Malaysian businessman, Ishak Ismail, the owner of all the Kentucky Fried Chicken franchises. "What is the great appeal of Kentucky Fried Chicken to Malaysians?" I asked. Not only did they like the taste, he said, but they liked even more what it symbolized — modernity, Americanization, being hip. "Anything Western, especially American, people here love." Today, for better or for worse, globalization is a means for spreading the fantasy of America around the world. In today's global village, people know there is another way to live; they know about the American lifestyle and many of them want a big slice of it.[1]

Let me give you another example. Everyone told me that I was crazy to contemplate opening a Ripley's Believe It Or Not! museum in Thailand. Who in Southeast Asia would be interested in seeing a collection of the weird and wonderful from around the world? Well, the answer is: almost everyone. What had always appealed to me, as both a child and an adult, was equally of interest to the people of Thailand, whose growing wealth was matched by an increased curiosity. Check out the Ripley's in Pattaya; it's full of Thai families enjoying the exhibits sourced from all over the world. Ripley's in Hong Kong is also doing great business.

Here are some points to consider when doing your preparations:

- **Start small:** To begin with, it's probably best to start with one venture. I started with two — media broker and office cleaner — but that involved working all hours and dividing my attention, which, with hindsight, wasn't necessarily ideal for a fledgling entrepreneur. Keep it simple. Take one good idea and run with it.

- **Consider a franchise:** As a franchisee, our group includes such well-known names as Burger King, Swensen's, Sizzler, Ripley's, Dairy Queen, Trader Vic's, Benihana and Marriott. What is a franchise? The easiest way to explain it is this: you pay a company a fee for the use of its products or concept and, perhaps, its trademark. You normally have to pay the company that owns the rights to the idea or product an upfront fee, plus a royalty for each sale. It's a business concept that is used in most countries today.

  Franchising is perfect for the first-time entrepreneur, as agreements can be granted for a single shop or store. The contract, normally for between 10 and 20 years, often has a development requirement, sales projections, and a time limit in which to achieve results. There are other benefits, too. Franchises enable you to gain access to information and technology that you would otherwise have to spend a lot of money developing. This is a quick way to benchmark your product or business. There are franchises everywhere you look — in the fashion business, car sales, opticians, hotels. Many of the ideas that are franchised have come from small investors or entrepreneurs and have been developed by others into major concepts. For example, if you look at three fast-food chains in Thailand today — Pizza Hut, McDonald's, and Kentucky Fried Chicken — all were started by small businessmen. They were the tiniest of businesses in the beginning, just an individual restaurant. Look at them today.

  If you believe franchising is right for you, then remember that putting your signature on a franchise agreement isn't a guarantee of success. Some products will work in certain markets, but others will fail. Franchising trends tend to follow international brands that have a proven track record in the United States, Japan, and Europe. These brands must be identified, and the correct market research carried out to identify the target market and the best areas for reaching that market. So when it comes to signing a franchise agreement, tread warily and do your homework.

- **Identify problems in the marketplace:** It's important to be aware of the dangers and pitfalls. Sit down and work out what the potential problems are. Have a good, hard look at your start-up costs, running costs, and the competition. Don't kid yourself that it will be easy. Talk to as wide a range of people as you can to gather comments, but remember that most people don't think and act like entrepreneurs. They are only too happy to explain why something won't work, because they're not comfortable with the idea of taking calculated risks. If you ask your best friend, he will probably tell you you're crazy to even contemplate chucking in your secure job. He will come up with 101 reasons for you NOT to do something (like sell pizza in Thailand).

- **Do your research:** Research comes in many shapes and forms and can start right at street level. When we research the location of a new pizza restaurant, we count the number of pedestrians and cars in the vicinity of the proposed restaurant. Then we have a close look at the numbers. Are these the sort of people who are going to spend what in Thai terms is a lot of money? It's all very well having thousands of people who regularly use a ferry crossing, but are they thousands of people with no money to spend? As they used to say about China in the 1970s and early 1980s, a billion zeroes equals zero. The old real estate adage —

location, location, location — will always be the most vital factor for any retailer. Another method is simply to take a company you admire and see what they are doing well. What opportunities are being created? People have bought land in the vicinity of our hotels. Their thinking is that if we have got our sums right, the value of the land is going to increase and business in the area will boom. You can call it piggyback research.

- **Think laterally:** Identify complementary business opportunities that could stem from your initial idea. If you are going to distribute wines, why not also distribute spirits? If you're going to build a hotel, why not include a shopping plaza to help offset the cost of the hotel? We have developed residential condominiums, shopping plazas, and office buildings to help increase the returns from our hotels. Our pizza restaurants and Swensen's are often located close by each other, so that we can use the same warehouses and delivery routes, and draw the same customers.

- **Determine the capabilities and resources required:** Who else are you going to need? The success or failure of your venture will depend on some of the first people you hire. Make mistakes with these key people and your career as an entrepreneur could be a short one. If you are going to start a cleaning company, you'll need a good supervisor. I was good at going out and getting the contracts, but I needed someone who could physically get the job done. Fancy résumés look great, but will the person you hire be any good in the front line?

- **Project financial dimensions:** How much do you need to get started? When will you be able to turn a profit? How much do you need to charge? My first ideas required very little money. With the cleaning company, all I had to buy was a broom, cleaning materials, and a waxing machine. Labor costs and raw materials were low. Always minimize your costs, especially when you're just starting out.

The early days can be pretty tough. The first rule is survival. How much do you need to make in order to pay the staff, pay your rent, and feed yourself? It's as simple as that. As your business evolves and becomes much more complicated, the numbers will get bigger but the fundamentals will remain the same.

Note

[1]   Thomas Friedman, *The Lexus and the Olive Tree* (HarperCollins, New York, 1999).

Rule

✦

3

You Won't Be Committed If You're Not Having Fun

To love what you do and feel that it matters — how could anything be more fun?
             — Katharine Graham

The secret of happiness is not in doing what one likes, but in liking what one does.
             — James M. Barrie

I f you don't enjoy your work, you won't invest the time and energy needed to make it a success. I don't know of any successful entrepreneurs who consider their work boring. For most, it's a stimulating and challenging game. It *has* to be, because many entrepreneurs also spend most of their evenings and weekends working.

Never work just for money or power — it won't satisfy your soul, please your family, or help you sleep at night. Believe in and be committed to your business more than anyone else. In the early days, I was able to overcome most of my shortcomings through the sheer passion and enthusiasm I brought to my work. It's far easier to do this when you enjoy what you are doing.

While Henry Ford worshiped the motor car and Bill Gates adores computer software, my passions are more varied. I happen to love pizza, ice cream and hotels, not necessarily in that order. I love to eat — European food, Asian food, American food — you name it. Thai cuisine is available almost everywhere in the world these days and Bangkok is now a gourmet's paradise. But when I was a kid, there was very little Western food available outside the smart hotels and clubs. I was particularly fond of pizza, so as an adult I relished the opportunity of making pizza available everywhere. For me, a great pizza is a wonderful meal. You simply can't beat it. I also love hot dogs, so we now sell those in our Dairy Queens.

It's the same story with hotels. They are a real challenge, as they call on many different skills — design, construction, budgeting, service, selling, and training. We have a reputation for building quality hotels with limited funds. The Regent in Chiang Mai is a six-star hotel, but it cost only a fraction of the price of its competitors around the world. That's quite a skill. The beautiful new Peninsula Hotel in Bangkok cost ten times what it cost to build the Marriott Royal Garden Riverside, which lies just 15 minutes downriver. Is it ten times as good? Will it get room rates that are ten times higher? You can guess which will have the better return on investment.

I believe that my early career in advertising helped me a great deal. Advertising teaches you a little about a lot of businesses: food, marketing companies, retailing companies, hotels, ice cream. You have to be a Jack-of-all-trades. But most importantly, you have to be interested in the subject matter. In the early days, when I was getting started, I really loved the media business, especially advertising. I used to wine and dine the clients, write the copy, do the creative work, make the presentations, and produce the television commercials. I didn't mind working crazy hours, because it was *fun*. I constantly ask myself, "Do I really want to be doing this? Is it enjoyable?" If the answer is "no," I re-examine the business.

I read a story recently about two young people who came to Asia with a background in the airline business. They wanted to work for themselves and looked around for business opportunities. At one stage they planned to start their own sock company! They knew next to nothing about socks, so it's not surprising they couldn't get passionate about the idea. They are now running an air taxi business, which makes a hell of a lot more sense. You'll get much more satisfaction if you go with what you know!

There are, of course, exceptions to every rule. It was the fast-food business that involved me in one venture that I couldn't wait to get out of. It was one of those deals that seemed hexed from the start. After lengthy negotiations, I obtained the license for the first Pizza Hut in Beijing on May 26, 1989. A few days later we remitted US$500,000 to China. The date was June 4 — my birthday, and the day the tanks rolled into Tiananmen Square. It was too late to back out, and we sat and watched in horror as the military crushed the student demonstrators before the world's television cameras.

The project was put on ice for a year. Even the Chinese agreed that this was necessary. They preferred to see the project delayed than canceled. At that time, many business people were simply walking away from deals. We eventually opened and, although the mood in China was very tense, the restaurant was successful and we were making money. However, I soon sold the business, because I simply wasn't enjoying the project. It was one of those deals that started off badly and never really got any better.

The authorities never wanted to talk to my number 2; they always wanted to talk to me. I would have to go up to Beijing every month, where it would take all day to decide whether we should buy a dish washing machine or install another sink. It was frustrating and a waste of time, a commodity I cherish dearly. We had a joint venture with the government — we had 60% and they had 40%. At times, I wanted to scream, "God damn it! We're going to do it *our* way!" But you just don't say that to the Chinese government. Instead, you have to search for a compromise. I believe the reason a lot of Asian joint ventures with Americans don't work out is because the Americans don't understand that business isn't always done their way in Asia.

Anyway, back in Beijing, life wasn't getting any easier. We were told the building didn't meet fire regulations. We were renting a building from the Beijing municipal government that didn't meet its own fire code! We were going to be thrown out of the building by our own partners! The staff wanted to go on strike, even though we were paying them three times the national minimum rate. I dreaded flying to China every month, where there was always another department to deal with. I simply lost patience with the partners and wanted out. It just wasn't fun anymore. This may be one reason why I'll never be one of the richest people in the world. Even though I might make a lot of money out of a venture I don't enjoy, I would rather have more time for my family and the businesses I do enjoy. So, we sold the Beijing Pizza Hut business. We didn't make much money, but we didn't lose any either. Most people who invested in China at the time ended up losing a fortune. I helped to pioneer fast food in China, but it wasn't a key part of our business and, though it was a shame to have to get out, I still believe I made the right decision. This experience aside, I have enjoyed being in the fast-food business. Today the Pizza Hut business I started is worth several hundred million dollars.

In addition to enjoying what you do, you must be fiercely committed to it if you want to survive. The fainthearted don't last long as entrepreneurs. Commitment is especially important early on, when you have a little bit of everything — a little bit of money, a little bit of business, and a little bit of a reputation.

In Bangkok in the early days of the advertising business, we were always competing against bigger names. For example, when we were a tiny agency in the 1970s, we were doing battle with the likes of Ogilvy & Mather, Lintas, and Ted Bates. We were pitching against them and sometimes beating them to big accounts they wanted, including Ford, Firestone, and Lever Brothers. Ogilvy wanted to buy us. We had clients telling anyone who would listen how good we were. A lot of that came down to our commitment and hard work, and the fact that we enjoyed what we were doing, especially if it involved tweaking the noses of the big international agencies. As it turned out, having a good reputation paid bigger dividends than we could ever have imagined.

One day our accountant ran off with most of our money. It was a major disaster, to say the least, and we were in great danger of going under. I went to our clients such as Ford, Firestone, and Singer and told them what had happened. I said, "The only way we can survive is if you are willing to pay us in advance." Our clients supported us and paid up. People knew we were totally committed. We weren't in it to make a fast buck and then get out of town.

But your level of commitment can't diminish as you become more successful. At the back of my mind I have always worried that tomorrow I could fail. You never have a chance to relax and just enjoy the spoils. You never reach a plateau. Don't think that when you are worth US$10 million you'll be able to sit back and say, "I have truly achieved success." By then, you might have thousands of employees who depend on you. The pressure just keeps mounting, so you are always on that treadmill. But if you are capable of staying in front, the energy that flows from an entrepreneur should inspire the senior staff. Entrepreneurs continually challenge themselves, which inspires others to try and keep up. The next challenge lies just around the corner; the minute you run out of challenges, it's time to retire.

Staying on top is damned hard work. Ask the management at Bangkok's Oriental Hotel, arguably the best hotel in the world. What is there after being number 1? You can be number 2 or 3, or you can fall off the list completely. Once you become number 1, how do you stay there? You have to come up with new ideas first. Don't let the competition beat you to the punch, even if they are big international players. KFC and McDonald's are sitting there right now thinking about how to steal more "share of stomach" from our quick-service restaurants.

If you really want to understand commitment, try surviving a crisis, especially one of the magnitude that swept across Asia in 1997. We survived, but many businesses in Thailand and elsewhere didn't. It was touch-and-go for a while and I had many sleepless nights as I watched the baht plummet against the dollar and interest rates rise to painful levels. The darkest moment came in January 1998, when the baht went past 55 to the greenback — it was 25 to the dollar before the crisis — and people were talking about it going to 70 and then 100.

A crisis like that really tests your commitment. The numbers became scary and we were losing millions of dollars. I'll discuss the great crash of 1997, and how we survived it, later, but there is no doubt that I was under more pressure and had to work harder than I had in years. All I can say is, thank God I enjoy what I do. It made all that pain worthwhile!

Rule

4

Work Hard, Play Hard

One hour of life, crowded to the full with glorious action, and filled with noble risks, is worth whole years of those mean observances of paltry decorum in which we steal through existence, like sluggish waters through a marsh, without either honor or observation.
— Sir Walter Scott

It is impossible to be successful at anything doing it part-time. If you spend 100% of your time to make $100, you can't say "I'll spend 90% of my time and expect to make $90." The money is made on the last 10% effort. It's like climbing Everest; the success of the expedition lies in the last 10%; the last bit of extra you give.
— Arne Naess

The lot of an entrepreneur isn't an easy one. When I work, I work very, very hard. As I work most of the time, this means there is a price to pay. The first casualty is your social life. What was mine like when I started? That's an easy question to answer: I didn't have one. There simply just wasn't the time. In the very early days, I would go out in a jacket and tie to drum up business for the advertising company by day, and then change into overalls to help clean offices at night.

As a teenager I rarely had a date, because I was always finishing work at 10 p.m. or later, which didn't impress the young ladies very much. I lost touch with a lot of my friends from the early days, too. Be warned, it can be a lonely life.

I managed, because I was lucky enough to have a wonderful woman in my life from the very beginning. My wife Kathy, whom I married when I was 18, is a saint in human form. She has put up with so much for so long that I cannot thank her enough. The sacrifices don't necessarily disappear as you grow older and, hopefully, more successful. I have missed my kids' softball games, birthday parties, and even their graduation ceremonies. Kathy has coped magnificently, but if I do have any regrets about the entrepreneur's lifestyle it is the time spent away from my family. You can only hope that they understand.

Often, the workload leaves a lot to be desired. The idea is to squeeze the clock and get the most out of every hour, every minute, of each day. Get the first flight out and the last flight back. Don't stay overnight in Hong Kong or Singapore if it's avoidable. It might be ten times more entertaining to stay over and have a night out with friends, but is it the most productive use of your time? Probably not. For me, the extra hours at home are more precious.

My mother lives in Thailand and describes our meetings — normally lunch at one of the hotels — as a series of brief encounters between business engagements. But she has always been there for me. So, never take your family for granted; they are your greatest asset.

Plan your day. I try to keep my schedule reasonably sane when I'm in Bangkok. On weekends I like to inspect one or more of our properties out of Bangkok.

My brother Skip says my idea of a fun weekend is to jump in the plane at 3 p.m. on Friday, fly to Chiang Mai, inspect our hotel and the condominium construction, attend meetings, have dinner, get up early the next morning and rush to the airport; fly to Pattaya, site-inspect the hotel, check out our entertainment complex, attend a meeting, have dinner at Benihana, get up early the next morning; fly to Hua Hin, cast my eye over our two hotels, have lunch with my mother, fly back to Bangkok and then start the week all over again. He exaggerates, of course. These days, I generally only fly to one place each weekend, but it's true that I like to combine business with pleasure.

There are compensations. I have found that the harder I work, the luckier I get. David Ogilvy, that great man of advertising whom I was lucky enough to work for, once told me: "A person who works 16 hours a day will get where he wants to go twice as fast as one who works eight hours a day." I have followed his advice on most matters, and he has yet to let me down.

OK, you've got the picture. It's hard work. But no-one can spend all their time with their nose to the grindstone. It's not good for the mind or the body. All work and no play tends to make you both a very dull person and less likely to be successful as an entrepreneur.

Play hard, too. If you are going to keep any sort of perspective on life, you must make the most of your precious free time. Leisure has always had a place in my heart. When I was a kid I loved to water ski and race go-karts, and before long I had graduated to fast cars. I broke the overland record from Singapore to Bangkok when I was a teenager. I have also raced regularly at the Macau Grand Prix with some success. Sports cars remain a great love of mine, and the garage at home has seen its fair share of Jaguars, Corvettes, BMWs, and the like.

Another great passion of mine is scuba diving. I started diving in Thailand and immediately fell in love with the sport. I have dived all over the world and have been eyeball-to-eyeball with whale sharks in Asia, hammerheads in Papua New Guinea, and Great Whites off the southern coast of Australia at a place aptly named Dangerous Reef, where some of the action sequences for the movie *Jaws* were filmed. You are taken out on a boat and then lowered into the sea in a shark-proof cage. Bait is placed in the water and you wait for the sharks to arrive for their free lunch. The results are spectacular. You can actually touch their heads as they press against the cage. I was so impressed by the experience that we included a video showing the sharks at their most ferocious in our Ripley's displays in Pattaya and Hong Kong. I am the first to admit that this sort of diving is thrill seeking, not real diving, but the experience of seeing these 18-foot monsters up close was unforgettable.

It is very difficult to beat swimming alongside whale sharks in the waters surrounding remote islands off Burma. These massive, graceful, harmless beasts are quite stunning. I usually dive with the same group of people. Being with good friends makes a wonderful vacation away from the phone,

e-mail, and fax. I have been known to be out of communication for as long as two weeks almost every year. This is
good for me as well as for my executives, who have to operate
without my presence.

Flying has now become more than a hobby, and I find it
both challenging and relaxing. Lining up in a six-seater Piper
Malibu behind a Jumbo on the runway at Bangkok's Don
Muang Airport is quite a buzz. I find flying a wonderful escape
from the stresses and strains of business life. The fact that I can
use the plane as a highly effective business tool makes it
doubly satisfying. A couple of years ago, I piloted my new
single-engine Piper from Florida to Thailand. It took 64 hours,
with a few stops along the way, compared with the usual 18
hours by jet, but I wouldn't have missed a single moment.

I think it is important to be always on the lookout for new
challenges, in your leisure time as well as your business. That's
why, in the middle of the Asian financial crisis, I decided to
learn how to fly a helicopter. For the first few hours I was
completely baffled. Piloting a helicopter is an amazingly
complicated business, and much more difficult than learning
to fly a light aircraft. It involves coordinating the use of both
hands — with a separate wrist motion — and both feet, all at
the same time. I signed up for lessons in September 1998 and
by early in 1999 I had made my first solo flight. It gave me a
tremendous sense of accomplishment and I am now the proud
owner of a helicopter pilot's license.

I would love to be able to boast that I am a natural all-
round athlete. That isn't the case, as I discovered to my cost a
few years ago. Having been a competent water skier, I thought
snow skiing would be relatively straightforward. It was a
disaster. I separated my shoulder on my first day on skis at
Lake Tahoe in California. It was very embarrassing, as I was on

the "kiddie" slopes when I fell. My punishment for my presumption was a six-hour wait in a clinic on New Year's Eve. Skiing and I have been strangers ever since.

Whatever your favorite sport or hobby, pursue it with as much passion and energy as you put into your business. As some wise person once said, "Only a busy person can truly enjoy leisure."

Rule

✦

5

Work With Other People's Brains

When you hire people who are smarter than you are, you prove you are smarter than they are. — **R.H. Grant**

The best executive is the one who has sense enough to pick good men to do what he wants done and self-restraint enough to keep from meddling with them while they do it. — **Anon**

M any entrepreneurs of the old school take pride in the fact that, despite an abbreviated education, they have accomplished a great deal through their experiences at the "university of life." But the modern entrepreneur faces a more complex world and needs a solid education. Don't let anyone tell you that a good entrepreneur doesn't recognize the importance of technical knowhow. In my case, I realized very early on that I needed qualified, experienced people, so I set about hiring them. However, superb academic qualifications, even from the most prestigious institutions, don't guarantee success at any level of the corporate world. Whatever the enterprise, you must either have the technical knowhow or be able to hire it. This is called "working with OPB" — other people's brains.

When I speak to young people, the message I try to send them is: don't drop out of school if you want to be successful in business. Times have changed. If you were thinking of going into a developing country like Vietnam to set up shop, you might still be able to achieve some success through sheer hard work and commitment, but if you are going to try to get started in a more developed market, forget it!

I had a serious disagreement with my parents about going to college. It had all been arranged: I was to be the first Heinecke to attend college in the United States. I even had a place at the University of Georgetown's School of Foreign Business Management. However, as the time of my departure drew closer, I was spending more time working for the advertising department of the *Bangkok World*, my local newspaper. My circle of contacts was expanding every week, and I felt I would miss out on too much if I left and went back to the States. Thailand in the 1960s was a land of opportunity;

it was also my home. I didn't want to spend four or five years studying and then come back and have to start all over again.

My father told me that if I didn't go to college I would never make anything of myself. As my mother is fond of reminding me, I responded that I was never going to work for anyone else, that when I needed someone smarter than me I would hire them, and that when I became a millionaire no one would give a damn which school I went to.

I think it was my mother's influence that prevailed. Her view was that if I thought I was so smart and wanted to work for myself, then I could do so without any help from my parents. Between them, they had an impressive network of contacts that would have come in very useful for someone in the advertising business. My mother also made it very clear that I should find my own place to live. I moved out within a month. I was 17 at the time.

The irony never fails to escape me when I look at the advice I gave my own kids. I told my two boys that if they didn't have a college education it was going to be difficult for them to get anywhere in life. Fortunately, they listened. Life was less complex when I started as a teenager selling ads for the *Bangkok World*. In those days, you could get to talk to the head of a multinational and he would say: "Sure, you can have an ad." Today, life isn't quite that simple. Things don't happen the way they used to. You can't get to the top person that easily, for instance. If I was starting out in Thailand today, I don't think I could make it by myself. For one thing, the costs are so much higher. I started with US$1,200; today, you would need a hundred times that, or more.

I learnt advertising from David Ogilvy, one of the most inspirational figures in world advertising. His advice to me, which I have never forgotten, was always to hire people who were smarter than I was. David Ogilvy was a fascinating man, an original thinker, an innovator, and a genuine eccentric. He had a huge influence on me and on my business philosophy. You have to love a man whose résumé when he started Ogilvy & Mather at the age of 38 read: "Unemployed farmer, former cook, and university dropout." He omitted to mention the time he spent working in the United States for George Gallup, creator of the Gallup Poll, as well as his stint with British Intelligence during World War II.

I met David Ogilvy through Michael Ball, the Vice Chairman of Ogilvy & Mather Worldwide, with whom I negotiated on the sale of my advertising agency. Michael and I had some lively discussions about the terms of sale and the final step required the approval of David Ogilvy himself. For this purpose, I flew to Paris for the day for an audience. I went to the Ritz to meet the great man. He spotted me in the bar and said, "You must be Mr Heinecke." As I thrust out my hand to greet him, he asked: "Are you married?" I nodded. "Do you love your wife?" he continued. I said I did, very much, and he replied: "Good. We like our partners to love their wives. It makes for a stable office environment." What I really wanted to ask was: "Do you love your second wife more than your first?" I didn't dare do so, of course, and it was probably a wise move, as the deal went through. I came to know Ogilvy well and to admire many things about him except his fear of flying. Sadly, David died recently at his beloved Chateau Touffou in France. I named my youngest son David after him — David William Heinecke. "William" is for me, an advertising talent who liked to think that on a good day he was sometimes in the same league as Ogilvy.

But I digress. Many people are smarter than me at many things — at writing speeches, at building a team, at patiently teaching the members of that team a new skill. It's the same story with finance. I had to learn rudimentary accounting pretty quickly when my first accountant ran off with all our money, yet I couldn't tell you the first thing about derivatives and I get confused by the ever-changing jargon of high finance. We have some very good brains who do that sort of thing far better than I ever will.

If you keep hiring people who are smarter than you in important areas, you will build an organization that is very strong. Outstanding companies such as Pepsi, Coca-Cola, IBM and Microsoft have outstanding people almost everywhere you look. I have a rather radical outlook on this subject. Hire great people and get them to work with you even if it costs you a lot of money. Compared to some of the people in our organization, I am way down on the salary scale. I have the most stock, but in terms of salary I have always paid myself only a nominal amount, far less than most of our key executives. I don't mind that they are making more money than I am, especially if they are doing their job well. Also, the fact that they know they are making more than the boss isn't a bad thing for morale. It's a very unusual arrangement in Thailand, but when there is someone I need badly who will bring something special to my organization, I pay whatever it takes to bring them on board. I look on it as a blue-chip investment; it's highly priced, but if it returns a good dividend it's worth it.

When I am hiring people, I don't pay too much attention to their résumé. A lot of my judgment is based on gut instinct. I look for people who I believe can drive a business, who display enthusiasm, who will treat the staff well. I want someone who is committed to developing talent. This is one of our group's core values. I'm not looking for entrepreneurs, as I don't want people too similar to me. Although I didn't go to university, I tend not to interview people who don't have a college education. I might have done so a few years back, when the company was smaller, but not anymore.

In the early days, I had a tendency to hire people too quickly. Someone came to see me for an interview, I liked what I saw, and I hired them. They were thrown in the deep end, and sometimes it worked out and sometimes it didn't. We are much more careful now, and the interviewing process is much more complicated. An applicant for a senior position today will be interviewed by at least six people — by me, two people from our human resources department, and two or three other senior executives. We try to ensure that we hire exactly the right people. One of my senior executives tends to hire only people with a Master's degree; she believes that it indicates both discipline and maturity. Specialist knowledge is the way forward these days, but never let too much knowledge blot out the creative spark. Let me explain.

To understand what an MBA does and what their limitations are, let's consider the life cycle of a typical Asian family business. Usually such enterprises are started by one person, with the spouse, children, and other relatives brought in to work long hours to help out. The business premises are often also the family home, so overheads are kept low.

The business succeeds because its basic concept is sound and also the entrepreneur's sense of timing is good. The entrepreneur is adaptable. If manufacturing plastic flowers isn't profitable, he or she switches to making wigs, then toys and electronics. Finally, the company finds a really successful niche and starts to expand.

The management style is based on common sense, and growth comes from natural momentum and intuition. But at some point there comes a sort of mid-life crisis. Orders aren't shipped on time, the inventory is out of balance, collections are late, and veteran employees become negligent and develop poor work habits. Fortunately, one of the founder's grandsons has recently graduated with an MBA. He is just what the company needs. He modernizes the operation by installing computers and improving management systems and controls. Collections improve, orders get shipped on time, and the business finds a new lease of life.

But what has to be appreciated is that an MBA could never have *started* the business. His degree is, after all, in business administration. He is an administrator, not an entrepreneur. It isn't the nature of an MBA to live in a factory, have his entire family work without pay, and to keep driving forward until the successful niche is identified. That takes an entrepreneur, a person of ideas, a "street fighter," not a structured systems expert.

Imagine the entrepreneur as a composer of music and the MBA as the conductor of the orchestra. While it is possible to teach someone to play an instrument or to conduct an orchestra, it is impossible to teach someone to be a great composer. A few years ago, *Fortune* magazine listed the hundred or so billionaires in the world. Of those who made their own fortune, as opposed to inheriting one, remarkably few had MBAs or, for that matter, any degree at all.

MBA graduates concentrate on things and systems, on the negatives, on correcting what is wrong — not on the positives, such as opening new markets, and finding new ways to serve customers and unique selling opportunities.

I have found that, like most people, MBAs concentrate on areas they understand, such as accounting, cost control and the like, and prefer to avoid involvement in research, product development, market innovation, and face-to-face selling — areas not taught in their course. The strength of MBAs lies in their ability to preserve funds. The entrepreneur's strength lies in coming up with ideas that generate cash flow. The former focuses on *cost* centers, whereas the focus of the latter is *profit* centers. So, embrace the specialist, but keep your creative juices flowing. You need each other.

I also think it is important to like the people you are working with. It makes the whole process much more enjoyable. My brother Skip is a good example. We have heated arguments, but I value his judgment and input. He brings a lot to the table, as do many of the people I work with. I am surrounded by people I regard as friends.

Bill Bensley, who in my view is one of the world's great landscape architects, and John Lightbody, a brilliant interior designer, have worked on our hotel projects for many years. Bill graduated with a Master's degree from the Graduate School of Design at Harvard and has worked on prestige projects all over Asia. He has taken landscape architecture to a new level. John, who has been in Asia for nearly 25 years, combines original thinking with the ability to work within budgets and deadlines — a most unusual combination for a creative force. Neither Bill nor John started working for us because we paid enormous fees, but the relationships have blossomed into great friendships which ensures that our hotels' garden and interior designs are considered among the best in the world. Paul Kenny, our Australian chief operating officer, is probably one of the top food people in the world. He has driven our business forward in the many years he has been with the company, and is one of my best friends.

If you work with people who are very bright in their own field and have diverse talents and backgrounds, you will develop a team of tremendous strength and depth. It is essential to be able to recognize real talent and to cultivate it. Using other people's brains is a real joy if you like the players in the team. Working with someone you actively dislike, on the other hand, can be a deeply stressful experience, even if they are very good at what they do. In my experience, it's just not worth the aggravation.

You can pay people a lot of money, but creative people often work because they like the project and the people involved, rather than just the pay check. Many are highly sought after and are wealthy in their own right. They can afford to pick and choose.

It's the same with legal advice. We have been advised by John Hancock, a partner at Baker & McKenzie, for years, and he and I have become good friends. I don't try to be a lawyer; instead, I get advice from someone who is one of the best lawyers available.

You will never regret the time you put into developing and working with great talent. It is people such as this who will help to make you a more successful entrepreneur.

Rule

6

Set Goals (But Go Easy On The "Vision" Thing)

Our chief want in life is somebody who will make us do what we can. — **Ralph Waldo Emerson**

The man who believes he can do something is probably right, and so is the man who believes he can't. — **Anon**

My first goal when I started my company was purely and simply to survive. Now I find that I am able to enjoy the luxury of setting daily, monthly, and annual goals. I even have a few five-year goals. Unless you have a set of goals, it is extremely difficult to achieve anything and to measure your progress. Goals drive you forward when you are in danger of resting on your laurels and help to focus the mind when times are tough.

But first, it is important to distinguish between goals and visions. They are very different, as the recent crash in Asia has shown. The vision thing — as former U.S. president, George Bush, put it so famously, if a tad inelegantly — can be dangerous in the wrong hands.

Thailand and much of Asia were awash with shattered visions in 1997. If you drove around Bangkok at the time, the city was littered with half-finished highrise office complexes and residential buildings. These were grandiose schemes aimed at a non-existent market. The financing of these developments was pure folly, part of the illusion of an everlasting middle-class housing boom which had in fact started to slow in the early 1990s. They were bricks made without straw, empty visions without a bottom line in sight. It is essential to strike a balance between vision and day-to-day reality.

The key is to look at things in the context of a very small idea. If it works, it is very easy to expand and grow. But you must first be successful. To build a wall, you start with the first brick and then carefully add more bricks. Sometimes you can't visualize how big a wall you are building. If I had visualized the wall that is our group today, I wouldn't have known where to begin. I don't think too far ahead. I feel sometimes that if you think too far ahead, then you get caught up in the planning rather than the doing.

It's one thing to say you want to be the biggest restaurant operator in the country. It's another to ensure that you are a profitable operator. Take it step by step, one restaurant at a time, just as we have done with our pizza restaurants.

Looking back at when we first started, we did not have a plan to build luxury hotels around the country. We began with a cluster of bungalows in Pattaya in 1978 and tried to improve what had been an old U.S. military R&R facility. We then built a second hotel, a third, and then a fourth, all in different parts of the country. It happened step by step. I didn't wake up one morning in 1978 with a vision that I was going to be one of the premier hotel operators in Thailand.

First, we had to learn the business, the nuts and bolts of running 30 bungalows efficiently, making a profit, and slowly building a hotel company. Years later, in 1998, right in the middle of the Asian crisis, we were able to make a successful pitch to buy a big slice of one of the ten finest hotels in the world, the Regent Bangkok.

Who would have thought that a little company that started with a few bungalows in Pattaya would be able to climb so high? I never had that vision. My goal was to operate a profitable hotel in Pattaya, and then a profitable hotel in Hua Hin, and then a profitable hotel in Bangkok. All our Thai hotels are not just profitable; they are possibly the most profitable in Thailand.

The process of taking things a step at a time works against the whole visionary concept. I am sure that if you asked people like Bill Gates at Microsoft if he set out to be the wealthiest man in the world, he would say "No." He started by aiming to produce the best software program he could.

Your business must be built solidly from the ground up. We didn't realize that our fast-food business would become so big. Little did we think that within 20 years we would have more than 350 restaurants around the country. That wasn't the plan; it wasn't our vision. You are only as good as the last pizza you sell.

In 1989, we set up a joint venture to make golf gloves in Thailand. The goal was to make it profitable and then to expand the production level. It is now the biggest producer of golf gloves in the world. You can think big, but remember to start small. Your goal should be to make your business a success; if you can do that, the money will come. Money is only a way of keeping score, a way of judging how well you are doing.

My business goals went back to basic survival mode in 1997 when the crash caught us exposed to a plunging baht and soaring interest rates. First, we had to survive, just as I had had to do back in the early days. After a few difficult months, we accomplished that goal and our survival was assured. Now it is time to set new targets. We would like to make our food group — which includes The Pizza Company, Sizzler, Swensen's, and Dairy Queen — a company with annual sales of US$500 million within five years. We had sales of about US$100 million before the crash and reached almost US$100 million in 2000. Again, we will build restaurant by restaurant, shop by shop, pizza by pizza, sundae by sundae. The fight with Tricon over the Pizza Hut franchise set us back on our heels in 2000 but the amazing success of The Pizza Company helped to put sales back on target to surpass the US$100 million mark in 2002.

We also hope the hotel group will become the leading hotel group in Thailand. With a world-famous company like Dusit Thani competing against us, it won't be easy, but we aim to give them a run for their money.

On a personal level, one day I want to own a vintage racing Ferrari, take some more motor-racing lessons, learn to fly a jet, and become a first-class helicopter pilot. Now isn't the time to buy a Jet — we are still rebuilding after the crash — but I can see one on the horizon.

Goals are about pushing yourself. I raced cars with a good deal of success, but I went to a motor-racing school to get better. There, I discovered that many of things I had been doing were wrong. You always have to be willing to learn. I had been driving go-karts competitively from the age of 13 and driving racing cars from the age of 17. At 44, I was still prepared to go back to school and learn new skills. I want to stay competitive, too.

The day you think you know it all in any field, you had better watch out. Just look at what the Asian crisis has thrown at us! The goal always has to be: let's see how we can be better than we were before.

A while back, I was reading about an expert who gave a speech on the subject of management. He was speaking to a group of business students and, to drive home a point, used an illustration those students will never forget. As he stood in front of the group of high-powered overachievers, he said, "OK, time for a quiz." He placed a one-gallon, wide-mouthed jar on a table in front of him and then produced about a dozen fist-sized rocks and carefully placed them, one at a time, in the jar.

When the jar was filled to the top and no more rocks would fit inside, he asked, "Is the jar full?" Everyone in the class said, "Yes." He asked, "Really?" He then reached under the table and pulled out a bucket of gravel. He dumped some of the gravel in the jar and then shook it, causing the gravel to work its way down into the spaces between the big rocks.

Then he asked the group once more, "Is the jar full?" By this time the class was on to him. "Probably not," one of them answered. "Good!" he replied. He reached under the table and brought out a bucket of sand. He started dumping the sand into the jar, where it filled the spaces left between the rocks and the gravel. Once more he asked the question, "Is the jar full?" "No!" the class shouted. Once again he said, "Good!" Then he grabbed a pitcher of water and began to pour it in until the jar was filled to the brim. Then he looked up at the class and asked, "What is the point of this illustration?"

One eager student raised his hand and said, "The point is, no matter how full your schedule is, if you try really hard, you can always fit some more things into it!"

"No," the speaker replied, "that's not the point. What this illustration teaches us is: if you don't put the big rocks in first, you'll never get them in at all."

What are the "big rocks," or goals, in your life? What is it that *you* want to accomplish? Is your goal to spend more time with your loved ones? Is it to focus on your faith or your education, or to improve your finances? Is there a particular cause that moves you? Do you really want to teach, or to become a mentor to others? Remember to put these goals in your life first, or you won't be able to fit them in at all.

Rule

◆

7

Trust Your Intuition

A great pleasure in life is doing what poeple say you cannot do.
— Walter Gagehot

Intuition is reason in a hurry.
— Anon

In business, decisions based on intuition are often superior to those based on analytical reasoning. You can pore over statistics, marketing reports, spreadsheets, and earning projections, but sometimes you just have to trust your instincts. *Intuition* is a difficult word to define. The Concise Oxford English Dictionary puts it this way: "Immediate apprehension by the mind without reasoning; immediate apprehension by sense; immediate insight."

In *The Book of Business Wisdom*, Igor Sikorsky, a brilliant inventor and aircraft manufacturer, described intuition thus:

> *It may be in the form of a fact or information held in the memory for which there is no data or known foundation but supported by a firm conviction that it is true. I always had a belief, even as a small boy, that I would sometime build and fly large flying machines. Consciously, I did not pay much attention to this idea because for many years I considered it simply impossible, but subconsciously the conviction was always there. Intuition works even when one does not recognize it as such. In other cases, it works with surprising speed and brilliance when, in a moment, a solution of a difficult and complicated problem comes in with remarkable clarity, and so convincingly that no doubts are left to its correctness.*[1]

In *The Book of Leadership Wisdom*, Walt Disney chairman Michael Eisner described how he was told on great authority by research and program analysts that the smash television hits *Happy Days, All in the Family, Roots*, and the movie *Toy Story*, wouldn't work.

> *I am not a disciple of research — unless of course it agrees with me. Otherwise, it is useless. Trusting one's deepest*

intuitions and instincts may mean overriding contrary research, peer pressure, conventional wisdom, or intimidation.[2]

Entrepreneurs prefer to call intuition a gut feeling or hunch, or to say they "just know" when something will work. For me, the secret is to avoid being stubborn and to listen with an open mind to what others say. I subject all decisions, whether they are the product of number crunching or of instinct, to searching examination. Then, at the end of the day, if that "feeling" is still there gnawing away inside my stomach, I trust my instincts. I have always relied heavily on intuition, and most of the time it has paid dividends.

For example, the idea to build a US$60 million shopping, entertainment, and hotel complex in Pattaya in 1991 raised many eyebrows and even a few laughs. Critics said that a new 300-room Royal Garden Resort and 50,000-square-meter Royal Garden Plaza shopping mall, including restaurants and the Ripley's Believe It Or Not! museum, would become expensive white elephants. After all, said the critics, Pattaya was famous for two things: prostitution and pollution. Red lights and raw sewage were unlikely to make a winning combination for such a big investment.

The *Asian Wall Street Journal* ran a long article headlined: "Believe It Or Not: Entrepreneur aims to turn Pattaya into family resort." But I looked at the project from a different angle. I spent half my time trying to convince people that Pattaya was a tremendously exciting market, and no-one believed it. I was telling anyone who would listen that Pattaya was a city resort that happened to be next to a beach.

I *knew* Pattaya. There was much more to the place than the seedy strip and a grubby beach. I had been going there since I was a kid, when my parents had a weekend home there. I had watched it grow from a backwater to a bustling city that was now only two hours' drive from Bangkok. (In the old days, it had been a six-hour journey.)

Also, I had cut my teeth in the hotel trade there more than 20 years ago. In 1978, I bought the old hotel that was built by the U.S. military for its troops on R&R leave during the Vietnam War. I had watched the Thai middle class spread their wings and become car owners and golfers in huge numbers. The road to Pattaya is now a highway, and the city is surrounded by excellent golf courses.

In terms of purchasing power, there wasn't another city in Thailand that compared. When people went to Pattaya, it was a spending experience. They wanted to be entertained, they wanted to eat, they wanted to go shopping. They were probably going to spend the night there, so they were going to pay for a hotel room.

That was the pitch, but at first the critics seemed to be right. We began building the complex in 1991 and the timing couldn't have been worse. The Gulf War broke out, there was a coup in Thailand, and a world recession was starting to bite. Undeterred, we pressed on and by 1995 the Royal Garden Resort and Royal Garden Plaza were open for business.

It was the biggest shopping plaza on Thailand's eastern seaboard, so there was an enormous amount riding on the project, not least my reputation. Well, it worked. The hotel, built on the site of our original investment, has been a huge success and, after a slow start, the retail space in the shopping plaza was fully rented out. Almost ten million people now visit the plaza annually. As for Ripley's Believe It or Not!, within a couple of months 50,000 people a month were pouring through the doors.

Why was it a success when so many factors were against the project taking off? The secret is that we offered families, both foreign and Thai, a package of activities in a convenient location. I trusted my intuition that Pattaya needed a major hotel and shopping complex at a time when most people considered it a bad investment. The result was that we built one of the most successful plazas in Thailand. I have always had a great belief in Pattaya. It is really a big city now. Numerous companies call this eastern seaboard area home, including Ford and General Motors. The hotel is now called the Pattaya Marriott Resort and Spa, and is going from strength to strength.

It was a similar story when we were planning our first hotel and shopping complex in Bangkok, the Royal Garden Riverside. Bangkok lies on the Chao Phraya river. Our plan was to build on the *other* side of the river, in Thon Buri, the unfashionable west bank, away from the city center where so many highrise luxury hotels are situated. "You must be crazy, nobody wants to stay there," was the general view. "You're going to have a lot of empty hotel rooms and retail space."

Well, the critics were wrong. Our view was that there were three main reasons why building on the other side of the river was a smart move. First, we would have the longest river frontage of any luxury hotel on the Chao Phraya. Second, we could build a beautiful low-rise resort in the traditional Thai style and set in lush, tropical gardens. I believed this would beat the hell out of staying in a highrise hotel room in the city. And third, guests had access to the city's leading attractions, such as the Grand Palace, by boat, which is the best way to travel in Bangkok with its traffic gridlocks.

The gamble paid off. The hotel opened in 1992 and is now an established part of the luxury hotel scene. The shopping and restaurant complex is also doing very nicely. We were the first to see the potential of the "wrong" side of the river, and have now been followed by the Peninsula, one of the world's great hotel groups. It's worth noting that their building costs were about ten times higher than ours and the hotel is a highrise. Today, our hotel goes under the name Bangkok Marriott Resort and Spa and remains a profitable and popular member of our hotel group.

That it pays to dare to be different is something I learnt a long time ago. In the early 1970s, when I first tried to sell pizza in Thailand, most people thought I was nuts. Thailand, they said, simply wasn't ready for Western-style fast food. Kentucky Fried Chicken had flopped in the 1960s and, anyway, Thais didn't like dairy products, particularly cheese.

Wrong. Thailand was ready and so was I. How did I know? Well, spending many years in Thailand helped, of course. Here's what I told an American newspaper correspondent in the late 1980s:

> *As an American I was looking at Thai society as an outsider and could see opportunities where others didn't. We believe that you do not adapt the product to Thai tastes but wait until Thai tastes adapt to international tastes. People are going to our restaurants to eat an American pizza, not a Thai pizza. They want to feel they're part of the new generation. As you see disposable income coming to Thailand you are going to see how similar not how dissimilar Thais are to every nationality in Asia and even Americans. They are all wearing a pair of Levis and using international cosmetics.*

And that was ten years ago ...

There are other examples. The same principle applied to Swensen's, the first really top-quality ice cream widely available in Thailand. I felt Pizza Hut would work in China. It did. When Pizza Hut started growing really quickly, I had a hunch it would be a smart move to secure a guaranteed supply of cheese, so we built our own cheese factory. When the baht plunged through the floor in 1997, you can imagine what would have happened to our Pizza Hut operations if we had been forced to import all the cheese. The hunch paid off.

No-one thought Chiang Mai was ready for a super-luxury hotel. After all, up until a few years ago, the city was backpacker heaven and the highest room rate in town was US$50. Our six-star Regent Chiang Mai opened in 1995 and has been doing great business from day one. It is regularly described as one of the most beautiful hotels in the world, and suites cost up to US$2,000 a night.

If I ever start to doubt the merits of trusting my intuition, I have only to recall one particular occasion when I didn't do so and any doubts disappear. I am still kicking myself for failing to grasp the opportunity to take over one of the most famous hotels in Thailand, the Railway Hotel in Hua Hin. The property was a gem, with a rich history and a superb beachfront location in the heart of this beautiful resort favored by the Thai royal family. The author Somerset Maugham stayed here during his sweep though Southeast Asia. The property also included a prized golf course, the first to be built in Thailand.

The hotel was owned by the state railway and by the mid-1980s was starting to look as if it were being run by people who knew more about trains than hotels. To our amazement, it came on the market. This was an opportunity not to be missed. We weren't big enough to go it alone, so we put together a group of powerful bidders which included the influential King's Private Property Office, the personal investment arm of the royal family, and several banks.

Our consortium decided to put in a good bid and easily won the day, but the devil was in the details. Who would run this showpiece hotel? We were tied up in another hotel project, and our other partners said they didn't have the experience to take on such a big venture. Thailand was going through one of its periodic economic wobbles, and suddenly it was time to put up the necessary financing. We dithered and decided to forfeit our bond, since none of the partners could agree to manage the place. The moment was lost.

I should have had more trust in my intuition. The Railway Hotel would have been a great acquisition, and I know we could have made it work. I spent too much time worrying about the details — Who would manage it? How would we raise the money? — instead of concentrating on the big picture. To make matters worse, the ultimate winners were rivals of ours, and I have to admit they have done a great job. It is now the Sofitel, and I kick myself every time I drive past what is still the most famous hotel in Hua Hin.

So, try to develop an awareness of your intuition and learn to trust it.

Notes

[1] Peter Krass (ed.), *The Book of Business Wisdom* (John Wiley & Sons, New York, 1997), p. 366.

[2] Peter Krass (ed.), *The Book of Leadership Wisdom* (John Wiley & Sons, New York, 1998), p. 439.

Rule

Reach For The Sky
(At Least Once)

The future belongs to those who believe in the beauty of their dreams.   — **Eleanor Roosevelt**

It is a funny thing about life; if you refuse to accept anything but the best, you very often get it.   — **Somerset Maugham**

Accept the challenges, so that you may feel the exhilaration of victory.   — **General George Patton**

Think big. Don't ever be afraid to take a bold step if one is necessary. You can't cross a canyon in two small jumps. Advertising guru Leo Burnett perhaps summed it up best when he said: "When you reach for the stars you may not quite get one, but you won't come up with a handful of mud either."

The ambition to succeed should be closely linked to the pursuit of excellence. These aims can be realized in many ways, both big and small. We can't all be Henry Ford or Bill Gates. My ambitions range from attempting to please every single customer in a fast-food restaurant, to building quality hotels that leave guests with a special memory. Exceed your customers' expectations and they will come back over and over again. Give them what they want and then do a little more. Let them know you appreciate them. Make good on all your mistakes and don't make excuses. Apologize when you have to, but stand behind everything you do.

As an entrepreneur, don't be afraid to take on the big boys. We have been doing that from day one. Our little advertising agency in the early days in Bangkok went head-to-head with Ogilvy & Mather, Lintas, and Leo Burnett for the accounts of international clients. We more than held our own. Don't forget that our Pizza Company, Swensen's, and Burger King franchises have been competing successfully against all industry giants such as Pizza Hut, Baskin-Robbins, and McDonald's.

The day-to-day battles demand a huge amount of hard work if you are to stay ahead, especially when you are starting out. But perhaps once in a lifetime — twice if you're lucky — you become involved in a project that lifts you above the daily grind of making your business a success and instills in you a desire to achieve perfection.

For me, that project of a lifetime is without doubt the

Regent Chiang Mai. This property, which opened in 1995, has always meant something quite special to me. It was born in a crisis and could have done my business serious damage if it had failed. Instead, it has become the jewel in our crown.

The Regent Chiang Mai was a hugely expensive undertaking and represented a substantial risk because no-one had ever built a top-class hotel in the northern capital of Thailand. Chiang Mai, the second-largest city in the country and the second most popular tourist destination after Bangkok, had long been associated with backpackers and trekkers attracted by the beauty of the mountainous terrain, the exotic hill tribes, and the city's proximity to the area known as "the Golden Triangle" — the bandit country straddling Thailand, Laos, and Burma where much of the world's opium poppies are grown. Even today, rogue warlords and thousands of their heavily armed followers control fiefdoms beyond the reach of any government.

Despite its size and location, Chiang Mai boasted nothing in the way of super-deluxe hotel accommodation. In the early 1990s, it was difficult to find anywhere to stay that boasted even a hint of luxury. The highest room rate in town was US$50. We felt that the time was ripe to open up this thousand-year-old city to the sort of tourist who would normally confine their activities to the best hotels in Bangkok or perhaps a very smart beach resort. "If we build it, they will come," was our thinking.

The plan was to build a good four-star hotel. We found a piece of land that had been a quarry; in its raw state, it didn't look like much. But the elevation of the site was superb, allowing fabulous views over the valley. Most people in the hotel business thought we had lost our minds. Why would we choose to get involved in such a project at a time when the tourist market had collapsed following an unusually violent coup and an economic downturn?

The corresponding dip in tourism and hotel room rates meant that our goal of attracting large numbers of people willing to pay a serious room rate was looking unattainable. As we had started building the hotel, we were left with three choices: cut our losses and bail out; plod on with the original concept and lose a lot of money; or rethink our approach. Confident that Thailand would recover its poise and always remain an attractive destination for well-heeled tourists despite the occasional coup, we decided to take a big gamble. We changed our strategy and chose to go way upmarket: we would create a hotel that would attract the sort of person who wouldn't blink at paying room rates they might expect to be charged in New York, Hong Kong, or Tokyo if we could provide an experience they would never forget.

The four-star hotel became five-star and, as luxury upon luxury was added, it soon became a member of that elite class, the six-star hotel. The project became so luxurious, in fact, that we invited our friends at the Four Seasons who owned Regent International to manage the venture. After a splendid lunch and a lengthy site inspection, they agreed to give it a try. At this point it was very clear to us that everything to do with this hotel had to be remarkable — spectacular in both concept and execution.

For the design, we went back to the thirteenth century. Chiang Mai was then the center of the agricultural Lanna empire ruled by King Mengrai. Influenced by its neighbors in China, Burma, and Laos, Lanna — which means "a million rice fields" — epitomized what is now regarded as classic northern Thai architecture centered around the elevated teak house. The strategy was to build a resort that combined

Chiang Mai's accessibility — it is only an hour from Bangkok by air — with its links to the past. To integrate historical integrity and modern comfort, we hired a traditional Thai architect, Professor Chulathat Kitibutr, and two great Western talents, designer John Lightbody and landscape architect Bill Bensley.

Our team then immersed themselves in what became a labor of love. Professor Chulathat, who lives in Chiang Mai, is recognized as Thailand's leading expert on Lanna architecture. He based the elegant two-story guest pavilions on upper-class Lanna homes found in a traditional northern Thai village. Each possesses its own *kaelae*, or intricately carved ornament on the roof, which denotes a high social rank. Another masterful touch was the introduction of a *sala*, or open-sided shelter, which allows guests to take advantage of the mountain views without leaving the privacy of their pavilion.

The pavilions are set in twenty acres of gardens featuring two small lakes, streams, waterfalls, and a working rice farm, complete with a family of water buffalo. At sunset, one of the forty gardeners comes by swinging his fire torch and lights the lanterns on the main pathway.

Inside, local teak is used extensively and the rooms are decorated with a rich array of northern Thai crafts, including celadon and lacquerware. Enclosed behind one of the baths and beyond the master bedroom is a secluded garden where carved wooden artifacts are set in a niche amid lush foliage. The modern touches include television, video, and airconditioning, as well as swimming pools, a health spa, and a tennis club.

The other theme we wanted to stress was sustainable tourism. The entire design is environmentally sensitive both in its use of materials and its seamless, low-density "fit" with the surrounding area. Nearly all the artwork and furniture is from the Chiang Mai region. Our investment in the local economy is highlighted by the use of local cottons, silks, and paper products. Hand-woven, naturally dyed cottons are used for the cushions, chairs, blinds, and uniforms.

The overall effect is magnificent and about as far away from a "modern" hotel as you can imagine. As Professor Chulathat pointed out, it was the first time that northern Thai traditions had inspired a resort hotel, and the irony was that it took Western developers to recognize their beauty.

This is how the hotel was described in the prestigious U.S. publication *Town & Country*:

Twenty minutes north of Chiang Mai, the stunningly original Regent has transformed magical northern Thailand from a region of backpacker hostels and business hotels to a place where soft adventurers can explore its unique hill country pleasure while cosseted in comfort. Monaco's Princess Caroline has already stopped in and it has become a popular weekend escape from Bangkok and Hong Kong. One plunges into the emerald scenery here as one would into a cool mountain stream. Cloud-wreathed mountains dense with jungle forests slope into celadon-green valleys threaded with lazy rivers; wooden temples embellished with carved wings harbor gleaming Buddhas, and wild orchids twine seductively through tangled branches.

Though the Regent offers all of the extravagant comforts one could wish for in a luxury resort, its real allure is its true sense of place. Staying here is a bit like taking a graceful step back into the 700-year-old history of the fabled Lanna kingdom, when Chiang Mai was the convivial crossroads of Burmese, Laotian, and Yunnan Chinese cultures. The Regent Chiang Mai is a new star in the luxury loop of world-famous Asian resorts.[1]

I must admit I glowed with pride when I read the review. It confirmed what we already knew — that we had created something quite special, a hotel that people would remember for the rest of their lives. At up to US$2,000 a day for a suite, they have every right to expect the very best. The hotel has been showered with awards from travel magazines, tourism bodies, and conservation groups. If I never do anything else, I will always have the satisfaction of knowing the Regent Chiang Mai is one of the world's truly great hotels simply because we dared to build it.

Our relationship with Regent has been a close one. The Chiang Mai hotel has been a financial success, so our partners and shareholders are happy. There is something about the Regent name that is very special. In 1998, in the depths of the Asian crisis, word leaked out that a stake in the Regent Bangkok was up for sale. It gave me another opportunity to be ambitious. The Regent in Bangkok is another fabulous hotel, one of the best city hotels in Asia, and it was a chance not to be missed despite the fact that the region's financial crisis was wreaking havoc on many aspects of our business.

As soon as I confirmed that the rumor was true, I called one of our directors, Anil Thadani who was previously a shareholder in the Regent Bangkok. In the space of about a week we put together an offer, and within two weeks we closed the deal, beating investment bank Goldman Sachs by only hours. We took 25% of the Regent Bangkok and, as the hotel owns a small share of Regent Chiang Mai, it has allowed us to increase our share in that splendid property too.

In 1999, more shares in the Regent Bangkok came on the market and we saw a chance to take a controlling interest in this world-class hotel. Unfortunately, we were not alone and this time Goldman Sachs used its enormous financial muscle to make an offer we couldn't match. The investment bank now holds 40% of the shares, so we are keeping some very grand company these days.

If anyone had told me 20 years ago that I would have been bidding against Goldman Sachs for control of one of Asia's great hotels, I'm not sure I would have believed them. I started with a few bungalows in Pattaya, and they led me to the Regent Chiang Mai. I had reached for the sky and created a star.

Note

[1] "The Kingdom and I," *Town & Country*, December 1997.

Rule

9

Learn To Sell

To convince others, first convince yourself.   *— Anon*

To sell well, dream well and tell well.   *— Anon*

My mother likes to tell the story of how I made my first sale at the grand old age of two-and-a-half when I set up a lemonade stand in front of our house in California. I'm not in a position to give you an accurate breakdown of the balance sheet for that particular operation, but my mother assures me I ended up in front. It just goes to show that whatever age you are and whichever business you are in, an entrepreneur must know how to sell. I don't know of any successful entrepreneurs who cannot sell themselves or their ideas. Indeed, chief executives are increasingly chief salesmen for their company.

But success doesn't come from just selling lemonade, pizzas, ice creams, or hotel rooms. It often starts with selling an idea, be it to your associates, partners, financiers, or the public. Selling is the ability to persuade people to see your point of view. I don't think I would be where I am today if I didn't have the ability to persuade people to come around to my way of thinking. "Let's give it a try my way, and if it doesn't work I'll try it your way" — that's my pitch. There must be a willingness to sell people on the benefits that can be derived from trying something your way. Selling is the art of persuading someone to give up one position in favor of another, and that someone can be a banker, a shareholder, or a customer in a fast-food restaurant.

How do you convince a client to give his business to your local advertising agency when he could go across the road to the rival operation that carries the name of an industry giant? How do you persuade a bank manager to lend you millions of dollars to build a hotel on the "wrong" side of the river? How do you persuade a bright young executive to come to work for you instead of for a big, international company that would probably pay more? How do you convince a dollar-conscious diner to buy an extra portion of garlic bread to go with their home-delivered pizza?

It all comes down to salesmanship. Some people are born with the skill; others have to learn it. The art of selling has been broken down by some analysts into five elements:

1. **Developing prospects**: identify what the customer wants.
2. **Making the approach**: begin by assessing the situation from the customer's point of view.
3. **Presenting the message**: believe in what you are selling.
4. **Closing the deal**: remember to get the sale. Anything else is just conversation.
5. **Following up**: make sure the customer is happy and wants to buy from you again.

Such an analysis is too complicated for me. I prefer to reduce the magic formula to just two ingredients: belief in the product, and enthusiasm. It's very difficult to sell something if you don't have much faith in it. For example, I am the agent for Cessna aeroplanes in Thailand. I have long admired these aircraft and believe them to be the best on the market. That makes for an easy and convincing sales pitch.

Without genuine enthusiasm, you'll be lost before you start. Years ago, I ran for president of the American Chamber of Commerce, the very organization that wouldn't allow me to join when I first started out because they said I wasn't old enough. My rival candidate was a banker who ran Chase Manhattan in Thailand. He was impressive in every way imaginable, both professionally and personally. The odds didn't look good, but my pitch was simple. I had been in Thailand for years and would be here for the rest of my life. My opponent was a typical expatriate who would be moving on in a couple of years. I had to make people believe that I was going to do a better job because I was much more committed to Thailand. The banker was a nice guy, but my enthusiasm, I believe, carried the day and I won the vote quite comfortably.

Belief and enthusiasm — these two magic ingredients often combine to good effect, as together they spell optimism. To sell, you have to be an optimist. The reason I can sell things and ideas to people is that I am always optimistic. This is why I have never had any difficulty selling Thailand as either a place to visit or in which to do business. One of the most successful speeches I have ever given was entitled, "What's Right about Thai Tourism?" The timing was interesting. It was May 1992 — just days after an outbreak of anti-government riots which saw the Thai military shooting civilians on the streets of Bangkok.

Here is an extract from that speech:

Thailand is known as The Land of Plenty — plenty of coups, plenty of traffic, plenty of pollution, plenty of prostitutes, plenty of flooding, and plenty of environmental problems. But Thailand has one other plenty — Plenty of Promise. Sure, we have problems — Aids, pollution, and infrastructure — but they are problems shared with many other international destinations. London, Los Angeles, Tokyo, Toronto, Rotterdam, Rome, Madrid, and Mexico City all have these same drawbacks to a greater or lesser degree.

I think it is time we, as business people and representatives of our individual countries, stop shooting ourselves in the foot on a daily basis by dwelling on the negative. We need to remind not only the rest of the world but ourselves as well that there is much in this country to be proud of and to share with our visitors.

Let's look at the bright side from a tourist's point of view. The Far East, and particularly Southeast Asia, remains one of the most exotic destinations to visit in the eyes of the rest of the world.

The international press coverage given to Patpong and Pattaya bars should be in the Guinness Book of Records *for the most disproportionate amount of press exposure per square foot of any place on earth. Thailand's extremely aggressive national Aids education program has been hailed by the World Health Organization as the most comprehensive of any country in the world. People constantly point out Thailand's negatives, but I am an optimist. I see the problems of the times being the opportunities of the times, especially for us in the tourist industry.*

People thought I was crazy to be so bullish, but I was proved right. Tourism in Thailand has continued to boom. *Of course it has.* How can tourism fail in a country that has Thailand's culture, beaches, shopping, food and, of course, its people? Merchants of doom never make particularly good salesmen.

I believe that every time you stand up and make a speech, you are selling yourself, your company, and your products. Most people, myself included, are not natural public speakers, but I would advise any entrepreneur to hone his or her skills as an orator. Think of the free publicity! Early in my career I took a course in public speaking and it was one of the best small investments I ever made. A word of warning, though: once you have some confidence in front of a microphone, don't get carried away. Accept the fact that very few of us are going to rival Winston Churchill as an orator, so keep your speeches brief, punchy, and relevant. Audiences will love you for it.

Also, never forget that pure hard work will always play its part in selling. Enthusiasm can often mean pure determination in the face of challenging circumstances. Making that extra telephone call, knocking on that last door, sending one more fax, all at the end of a long day, isn't easy, especially when you are not getting the results you want.

U.S. President Calvin Coolidge hit the nail on the head when he said: "Nothing in the world can take the place of persistence. Talent will not; nothing is more common than unsuccessful men with talent. Genius will not; unrewarded genius is almost a proverb. Education will not; the world is full of educated derelicts. Persistence and determination alone are omnipotent."

There aren't many successful salespeople around who are not both persistent and determined. History gives us some stirring examples:

- In his first year in business, Henry Ford went bankrupt. His second company also failed, but his third changed the world.
- In 1903, King Gillette invented the safety razor but sold only 51 razors and 168 blades.
- R.H. Macy went bankrupt with his first three stores.
- Howard Hughes, Sr., was forced to abandon his first oil well because he couldn't drill through the hard rock. He then founded Hughes Tool Co. and invented a rock drill that became the foundation for the family fortune.

On occasions, I have felt as if I have been trying to drill through rock with a blunt drill. In the late 1980s, I tried to put together two deals that tested my selling skills to the limit. A big American group was on the lookout to build a factory to make golf gloves in Asia. Golf was booming all over the world, especially in Asia, and although I was not a golfer at that time I knew enough to realize that the idea would work. The Americans had done plenty of business in South Korea and were keen to build there because they already had good business connections in that country. To them, Thailand was an unknown quantity and they were extremely apprehensive. I was so confident that the idea was a winner, I made them an offer they couldn't refuse. I told them I would buy the land, build the factory and lease it to the joint venture, and arrange the myriad permits needed. In the end, they came round to my way of thinking. It was a fine investment for all concerned. We invested less than US$200,000 and sold out for a package that approached US$8 million in 1999. The Americans had obviously forgotten how determined I was — their first buyout offer was only US$2 million. The final figure was reached after negotiations that can only be described as character-building.

The second tough deal revolved around the land for the Marriott Royal Garden Riverside Hotel in Bangkok. Having decided to go against the trend and build on the less developed bank of the Chao Phraya river, we then found a perfect piece of land. There was only one problem: it belonged to the Wanglees — one of the great Thai-Chinese families of Bangkok — who had owned the land for more than a century. It wasn't easy to persuade them to lease us the land for a small annual fee. First, they didn't need the money; and second, if they *did* want to part with the land, it would make more sense and a lot more dollars to sell or lease it to one of Bangkok's many large land-hungry developers.

I was basically saying, "Lease me your valuable land for a

small annual fee and trust me to build a successful hotel in a part of Bangkok where people don't build hotels. And another thing, let me mortgage the lease so that I can raise funds to construct the hotel." Well, we knew the family and they liked doing business with people they were comfortable with. They agreed to the deal. The hotel was a success, the family receives a good annual return on a piece of once-fallow land, they are regular visitors to the hotel's excellent restaurants, and we are still good friends.

A more recent example of a difficult sale was when I had to find millions of dollars to buy 25% of the Regent Bangkok during the darkest moments of the Asian crisis. Bankers were terrified of making big loans at the time, so we had to convince an investor (my old friend Anil Thadani of Schroder Capital Partners) that this was a rare opportunity to get our hands on a world-class property that would increase our revenues and make our company stronger.

If you doubt your ability to become a top salesperson, let me tell you the story of Jim Koch, the American who invented Samuel Adams beer and founded the wildly successful Boston Beer Company. In the book *What's Luck Got To Do With It?*, which describes the defining moments in the careers of a number of successful entrepreneurs, Jim's transformation from consultant and part-time brewer to master salesman is described as follows:

> *The longest walk he ever took was the 50 yards from his office, where he was a high-powered consultant, to the nearest bar, where he was just another beer salesman. He had talked to his uncle — a partner at Goldman Sachs and one of his backers — and the conversation had shaken him up. He told his uncle that he had been out*

shopping for a computer to keep track of sales to customers but then had to admit that he still had no customers. "So what the hell are you doing buying a computer?" his uncle barked, as he reminded Jim that many more businesses had gone broke because they didn't have customers than because they had no computer. At that moment, Jim, who felt that he was born to be a brewer, realized that he had better transform himself into a salesman. Jim approached the man behind the bar and started to make his pitch, only to learn that the man was not the bartender. Out came the manager, eyeing Jim suspiciously, and asked him what he wanted. Jim told him about Samuel Adams, opened his briefcase and poured out a glassful. The manager looked at the beer, sniffed it, drank it and immediately ordered 25 cases. For Jim, "It was an amazing feeling. In the space of 10 minutes I went from sheer terror to ecstasy."[1]

At that moment, a salesman was born.

Note

[1] Gregory Ericksen, *What's Luck Got To Do With It?* (John Wiley & Sons, New York, 1997), p. 49.

Rule

✦

10

Become A Leader

Leadership is the ability to get other people to do what they don't want to do, and like it. — **Harry Truman**

F ine words indeed, Mr. President, but easier said than done. Another man who sat in the White House, General Dwight Eisenhower, used to demonstrate the art of leadership with a simple piece of string. He would put it on the table and pull, and the string would follow. Then he would push and the string would go nowhere at all. It is the same when it comes to leading people. Effective leaders know that they get the best efforts out of people by working with them, by helping them to do their best, and by showing them how to be more productive.

David Ogilvy made these comments about leadership:

Great leaders almost always exude self-confidence. They are never petty. They are never buckpassers. They pick themselves up after defeat. Great leaders are always fanatically committed to their jobs. They do not suffer from the crippling need to be universally loved. They have the guts to make unpopular decisions — including the guts to fire non-performers. I do not believe that fear is a tool used by good leaders. People do their best work in a happy atmosphere.[1]

I also share Ogilvy's view that the man who had the wisest things to say about leadership was Field Marshal Montgomery:

The leader must have infectious optimism and the determination to persevere in the face of difficulties. He must also radiate confidence, even when he himself is not too certain of the outcome. The final test of a leader is the feeling you have when you leave his presence after a conference. Have you a feeling of uplift and confidence?[2]

This is indeed a good litmus test. I have had the privilege of listening to some great leaders speak in public, including Desert Storm chiefs General Norman Schwarzkopf and General Colin Powell. Within seconds of them starting to speak, I knew they were natural leaders. They exuded an aura of command. The same goes for Singapore's senior minister, Lee Kuan Yew. When I heard Mr. Lee speak, I knew I was in the presence of someone who was on a different level to the rest of us. I don't necessarily agree with everything he has to say, but there is no doubting his leadership ability.

Each leader has his or her own style. Tommy Lasorda, the legendary baseball manager of the L.A. Dodgers, once said that a leader was someone who walked out in front of his people but didn't get so far in front that he couldn't hear their footsteps. He is right. It is a question of striking the right balance between listening and leading. Don't create an atmosphere in which people are too timid to speak up and voice their opinion. They could save you from disaster.

Anand Panyarachun, the former prime minister of Thailand and one of the country's truly great leaders, put it this way:

> *I always emphasize that I want honest even though contradictory opinions from various cabinet members. I want honest, independent thinking. You have a right to have your own say. You have a right to disagree with the prime minister. You have a right to disagree with the cabinet decisions. But once a cabinet decision is made, you have to abide by it.*[3]

Quite. The same applies in business. Listen to those people whose opinions you value, but once you make up your mind, that's it. I do *not* believe in industrial or corporate democracy. The smaller the company, the more important this rule is. Without question, you must delegate responsibility and authority to executives and department heads. It's these people who make the company run. But never make the mistake of trying to run a company by committee. There is no question in my mind that a successful entrepreneur runs a dictatorship when it is called for — a company where things happen because he or she decides what should happen and when.

An entrepreneur is a leader who makes decisions — but they aren't necessarily always right. You will make your share of mistakes, but you should expect to do so unless you are passing your decision-making responsibility on to others and not showing strong leadership. If you are indecisive, your staff will know immediately. Don't be afraid to take risks or to be criticized. If you don't want to be criticized, you shouldn't say anything or do anything — but you also won't achieve anything. If I am going to fail, at least I want to know that it was *my* decision, and not someone else's which I had doubts about in the first place.

While leadership can be an elusive quality to define, there are some basic nuts and bolts which go to make up a useful platform on which to build:

- **Motivate**: Everyone has an invisible sign hanging from their neck that reads: "Make me feel important." Never forget this. You must make people understand the importance of what they are doing. You can't always make them perform better by offering more rewards, but you can make them more effective by stressing the significance of the job they are doing.

- **Listen**: You have to be a good listener. You have to be able to ask the right questions and create a climate of participation. It's surprising what people can contribute if you create the sort of atmosphere where staff feel absolutely free to come up with ideas. One of the best questions a leader can ask is: "What do you think?"
- **Trust your team**: If you don't believe in them, they are unlikely to give you 100%. Delegation involves trusting others, but it doesn't mean abrogating responsibility. When you delegate, you must accept responsibility for that action.
- **Say thanks**: Many managers don't seem to realize the power of those two simple words, "thank you," when a job is done well, especially when they are said sincerely.
- **Be courteous**: Again, this is so obvious that it should hardly need saying. However, it does. A cheerful, kind, and positive demeanor is a huge asset. There is no room for malicious and moody managers in my organization.
- **Keep your ear to the ground**: This will help you to spot a looming staff crisis before it happens. An article in the *Harvard Business Review* once described how a group of workers and supervisors had harbored grudges against management for 15 years without management being aware of it.
- **Be flexible**: Recognize that even the most committed people do have a life outside of work. Taking too many chunks out of even the most loyal staff member's leisure time isn't a smart idea.
- **Stay cool under pressure**: If the boss looks as if he or she is losing his/her head in a crisis, how do you expect the rest of the staff to respond?
- **Lead by example**: Be the first into the office and the last

out, especially when times are hard. Be visible. People notice and respond.

- **Be an expert**: Make sure that your staff know that you know what you are talking about.
- **Stay humble**: Never get too big for your boots; your customers are more important than you are.
- **Have a sense of humor**: If you don't have one of these, pack it in and go home now.
- **Celebrate**: When the news is good, don't be afraid to bring out the champagne.

In addition to these guidelines, I am a firm believer in "when in Rome ...". Each country and each market is different. For example, in Thailand and much of Asia, more importance is placed on developing a personal relationship and building trust with partners and staff than is usually the case in, say, the United States. With Thais, you have to know when to push and when to back off. I would say it took me at least ten years before I began to understand the great cultural differences.

Back in the 1970s, we had a run of bad luck. A warehouse burnt down, an employee died, and a senior member of staff quit to start up a business in competition to ours. The Thai staff saw a deeply disturbing trend emerging. The company was bad news. I tried doing everything the Western management handbooks recommended, but nothing worked, so I turned to the Thai way. We invited a dozen Buddhist monks to make offerings and bless the company headquarters, and we built a new spirit house. Our luck changed and the staff were happy.

I'm always interested to hear what other entrepreneurs have to say on the subject of leadership. Joanna Lau is a classic example of the migrant success story. Born in Hong Kong, she moved to the United States when she was 17. Her first job in a New York sweatshop lasted three days, as she couldn't sew. Joanna became a computer engineer and studied for her MBA at night. During the course, she prepared a case study on a defense contractor in Massachusetts that was in trouble. At just 30, with no hands-on experience, she decided to buy the struggling company. Within five years, she had turned a firm losing US$7 million a year into a profitable operation. How did she do it? By being a great leader.

"I always thought I would go into business for myself, but you don't really know when that will be," she said in *What's Luck Got To Do With It?*

> *When I was doing the case study I asked myself: If this were my company, what would I do? What could I do to make it work? What is the missing ingredient that I could bring to the table? I interviewed people across the spectrum of the company and I learnt that they really enjoyed what they were doing and they were giving 110 percent.*
>
> *Why would anyone provide money for someone who had never run a business before? It comes down to people. I made presentations to the employees and particularly reached out to the company's top executives. If they were willing to stay, I would then have an executive team behind me when I went for financial support. That is part of the reason why I share ownership of the company. I need[ed] to give them a percentage of the company so they would have a stake in it.*
>
> *I remember one of the senior executives, who had been with the company more than 20 years, saying to me:*

"What if you don't like me and one day you decide to fire me?" I answered that it was not a matter of liking someone or not but I was asking him if he wanted to be part of the team. Here was a chance to own a piece of the company. He agreed to stay, and I can tell you, if he hadn't I wouldn't be here today.

Here was I putting on the line my personal savings of US$401,000, a second mortgage on my house, my best years and I was walking away from a job where I was doing well and had good potential. That was persuasive. I was risking 100 percent and I was saying to them: "I'm willing to risk everything. You can join me or not." The good news was they stayed.

I'm like a conductor, putting a symphony together. As a conductor, all you need to know is what kind of music you want to play. Then you find the right instruments and players and continue to fine tune until you play beautiful music. That's the way I look at my job. You have to be honest with the people you work with and I think I've been honest with them about what I bring to the party. When I came in, I made it clear that I didn't know anything about running a business. But I was willing to give it a try and learn and pay the price. What you need to do is recognize your strengths and weaknesses and then fill in the gaps. I think we built a team and that was crucial in convincing key employees that we could make things happen together.[4]

LAU Technologies, as the company became, went on to win an award for excellence from the U.S. military for important work during Operation Desert Storm. The company re-engineered the circuit card to solve a safety problem in the turret drive of the Bradley armored personnel carrier. The job was done in 75 days instead of the projected 345.

This success story shows what good leadership can do, especially in a crisis. The recent problems in Asia gave many people the opportunity to show great qualities of leadership. I will deal with this in more detail in a later chapter, but suffice to say that not everyone displayed the same qualities of leadership as Joanna Lau, a rookie leader who showed that where there's a will to win, there is always a way.

Notes

[1] Peter Krass (ed.), *The Book of Business Wisdom* (John Wiley & Sons, New York, 1997), p. 110.

[2] ibid., p. 113.

[3] The Performance Group, *The Keys to Breakthrough Performance*, Bjelland, Dahl and Partners, p. 67.

[4] Gregory Ericksen, *What's Luck Got To Do With It?* (John Wiley & Sons, New York, 1997), p. 64.

Rule

11

Recognize A Failure And Move On

You grow older and wiser. In the early days you take every failure personally. But your skin thickens with age and you become more inclined to learn from your mistakes. — **Cheong Choong Kong**

Failure is often simply an unexpected situation that requires transforming into something positive. Don't forget that America is the result of a huge failure. Columbus was really looking for a route to Asia. — **Eugenio Barba**

I believe a characteristic of successful entrepreneurs is their ability to spot a disaster early. Don't let pride or sentiment affect your decisions. When an idea fails, use it as a learning experience and move on quickly to the next project. Don't be afraid to fail. It's one of the ways you learn to do things right.

I have always felt reassured by the fact that Babe Ruth struck out 1330 times, but he also hit 714 home runs. Ray Meyer, the legendary basketball coach at DePaul University, led his team to 37 winning seasons. One year, when his team lost after 29 victories at home, he was asked how he felt. "Great!" he said. "Now we can concentrate on winning rather than on not losing."

For many people, the word "failure" carries with it a sense of finality, but for the successful leader, failure is a beginning, the springboard to renewed efforts. Leaders simply don't think about failure. It's a bit like learning to ski. If you aren't falling down, you're not learning. I like the story about the promising young IBM executive who lost the company several million dollars on a deal that went wrong. Thomas J. Watson, IBM's founder, called the executive into his office, and the young man blurted out: "I guess you want my resignation?" Watson replied: "You can't be serious. We've just spent millions of dollars educating you!"

Walt Disney chairman Michael Eisner put it this way:

A company like ours must create an atmosphere in which people feel safe to fail. This means forming an organization where failure is not only tolerated but fear of criticism for submitting a foolish idea is abolished. If not, people become too cautious. Potentially brilliant ideas are never uttered and therefore never heard. Failing is good as long as it does not become a habit.[1]

It drives me crazy when I find out that a manager hasn't put an idea to me because he feared I would reject it. I tell my staff that the worst thing that can happen is that I will simply say "no."

The last impression I want to give is that everything I have ever touched has turned to gold. One of my earliest failures in Thailand was the early introduction of vending machines. Another was trying to duplicate in Malaysia the success of the Mister Donut fast-food franchise in Thailand. In both cases, decisions to write off hundreds of thousands of dollars were made in a matter of minutes based on results of activities that were less than a year old. You are looking at the man who became a "name" at Lloyds of London in 1990, just as everything at the insurance giant was turning sour. It looked like such an easy way to make money — just sign here and wait for the dividends to roll in. At least, that's what my friends who had made money told me. A string of natural disasters meant investors were liable for massive insurance claims. I lost every penny of my £250,000 investment. It just goes to show that there is no easy money in life.

Entrepreneurs should enjoy what they are doing too much to worry about failure. They are walking the leadership tightrope and should be more concerned about the opportunities that are missed by not even realizing they are there. As Wayne Gretsky, the great ice hockey player, once said: "You miss 100% of the shots you never take."

I am as guilty as the next man of missing out on great opportunities. Which entrepreneur turned his nose up at the chance to market running shoes? Me. I just didn't see it. I thought Thailand was too hot and Bangkok too polluted. The concept of Thais jogging for pleasure struck me as highly unlikely. Of course, I didn't think for a moment that running shoes would also become a fashion statement.

It was the same story with convenience stores. Some American executives came to see me about launching 7-Eleven in Thailand. I thought that, with thousands of tiny mom-and-pop shops operating all over the country, they must be nuts. How wrong could I be? The executives whom I chased out of my office then went to see the CP Group, one of the biggest companies in Thailand, and there are now hundreds of 7-Eleven stores in Thailand.

If it is any consolation, and it is to me, many others have messed up big-time. Consider the following:

- *I think there is a world market for about five computers.*
  Thomas Watson of IBM.
- *Television? No good will come of this device.*
  C.P. Snow, English author and journalist.
- *The Americans have need of the telephone but we do not. We have plenty of messenger boys.*
  Sir William Preece, chief engineer of the General Post Office in Britain.

And then there is the brilliant idea that is absolutely certain to change consumer habits. In 1988, one of the U.S. tobacco giants, R.J. Reynolds, decided the time was ripe to produce a smokeless, safer cigarette. Good idea, you would think, as the campaign against smoking was really getting into its stride, especially in the U.S. After spending millions of dollars on research, Reynolds came up with Premier, a "flavour capsule" that released the taste of smoke and nicotine. Great idea. Well, up to a point. Each pack came with a four-page book of instructions, the cigarettes were difficult to light, and were even more difficult to inhale. To cap it all, they tasted awful and smelled even worse. While Reynolds preached the benefits of the reduced health risks, smokers went back to their regular brands. Hindsight, as they say, provides 20-20 vision.

But even with the benefit of hindsight, some failures are easier to explain than others. In the 1960s, very early on in my career, I launched Vendasia, a scheme to bring soft-drink vending machines to Thailand. The theory was fine, but the one-baht coins vital to the whole operation kept changing size and weight. It was a disaster and I lost a lot of money, but it did teach me a valuable lesson: the importance of timing. Thailand wasn't ready for vending machines. Of course, the country is covered in them now and our coinage is rather more consistent. You can have the best idea, but if you are too early you can lose just as much money as if you are too late.

The Mister Donut failure in Malaysia still baffles me. The concept worked well in Thailand. The sweet flavor appealed to Thai tastes, as did the American "feel" of the shops. In the 1960s, Mister Donut had more outlets in Japan than McDonald's. I thought any American product that can do well in Japan has to be a great product, because Japan is a very difficult market for American companies. And anyway, I love donuts, so it seemed like a perfect fit and we were successful in Thailand from day one. People just loved it.

I suppose the failure showed the other side of the "borderless" coin — some things simply don't work in other places. It's not that we didn't try. We changed the locations, spent money on advertising, and experimented with the marketing. Nothing worked. The Malaysians wouldn't eat donuts — well, not my donuts, anyway. In the end we just called it a day, packed our bags, and went home.

Sadly, my string of failures doesn't end there. Another

spectacular flop was my attempt in the 1970s to run supermarkets. I bought the Thai operation of Hong Kong-based Dairy Farm supermarkets. The prospects looked good and for the second store we secured a lease on Sukhumvit, the road in Bangkok where, in those days, nearly all the foreigners and many wealthy Thais lived. What could be easier? The foreigners wanted all sorts of items they couldn't buy in local shops, as well as the airconditioned convenience of doing all their shopping in one place. The Thais were starting to get interested in the idea of supermarkets and were happy to try something new. What could go wrong? Just about everything.

The first thing you learn in the food business is that you have to be right every day. It's no good saying, "We had fresh milk yesterday." You are only as good as the last time somebody came into the shop. If you fail to have the item a customer wants, he will ask: "Why am I shopping here?"

I also underestimated the opposition. We were beaten hands-down by a Thai businessman who ran a store called Villa. He has gone on to great success in Bangkok and still runs the best supermarket in town. He deserves to have prospered, as his supermarket always had everything fresh, which was very difficult in those days. You had to know how much to order. Too much, and you were left with piles of rotting produce; too little, and you had a shop full of angry customers. Again, it sounds simple and obvious, but in practice it was very difficult. Another key part of the equation was finding reliable suppliers, which was very tricky back then.

I knew we were in trouble when my wife told me her friends preferred to shop at Villa, which was a nice way of saying that so did she. Villa's range of goods was better, and they were never out of stock. Your toughest critic is often someone like your spouse or your best friend, but they are doing you a huge favor by being frank. They were right: the opposition was better.

We got out as soon as we could, poorer but wiser. It's important to know when to cut your losses. The determination and perseverance I so admire can quickly become a millstone around your neck if you don't know when to stop throwing good money after bad. Never confuse qualities of determination with those of stubbornness and stupidity.

Despite everything I have been through, I am still making mistakes today. My most recent failure is Chicken Treat, which was launched in 1999 to help expand our fast-food business. Chicken is immensely popular in Thailand so it seemed a sensible, logical step. We believed we had a product that was every bit as good if not better than KFC, the market leader. So how could we fail? The answer is quite easy.

Looking back, we made all the classic mistakes. We built too many outlets too quickly before we knew exactly how the product would be received by the consumer. We then spent a lot of money on advertising a product that was still being refined. The result was that we never got it quite right despite having the right locations and our excellent delivery service.

Why didn't it work? Two reasons spring immediately to mind. The first is that in Thailand the chicken you can buy on the street — *gai yang* — is probably the best in the world. Roadside vendors cooking chicken on a makeshift grill, each with their own secret marinade, are a familiar sight around the country. Sold with sticky rice and spicy sauces, chicken is a delicious and cheap meal. Simply put, the competition is very, very tough.

The second reason is more subtle. The Thai fast-food market is changing. Ten years ago Thais craved all things Western. That is one reason why pizza was such a big hit.

Times are changing and Thai flavors are coming more into fashion, even in fast food. A growing sense of national pride is having an impact in many places, including restaurant menus. For example, McDonald's now sells a porkburger that consists of two pieces of sticky rice with a piece of pork in the middle. When McDonald's started selling a papaya salad — a Thai national favorite — it became a political issue and a major story in the press. How dare a foreign fast-food chain sell our national dish? roared the critics. It has been a big hit for McDonald's. It is worth noting that Jollibee outsells McDonald's in the Philippines because it caters completely to local tastes. We have changed too. We now have more Thai dishes on our menus, including a *tom yum goong* flavored pizza.

With Chicken Treat, we didn't get it quite right to begin with and by the time we did, it was too late to get the customers back through the door. From a high of 20 stores, we are now down to five. We will have to rethink our strategy if we are to make Chicken Treat work. We are not going to give up on chicken just yet. We have spent too much time and money and learnt a lot about the chicken business in the process.

The irony, of course, is that Chicken Treat was one of the major issues that triggered the battle with Tricon over Pizza Hut. Chicken Treat has not taken off yet, but The Pizza Company, the product of that battle, has been a smash hit. That's business for you!

Note

1   Peter Krass (ed.), *The Book of Business Wisdom* (John Wiley & Sons, New York, 1997), p. 440.

Make The Most Of Lucky Breaks

Success is simply a matter of luck. Ask any failure.   **— Anon**

Luck is what happens when preparation meets opportunity.
         — Elmer Letterman

L uck is being in the right place at the right time. Perhaps the most common trait found in lucky people is that they make the most of all the opportunities that present themselves. Good fortune isn't something you should wait for, but something you must seize. Napoleon once said: "Don't send me brilliant generals, send me lucky ones." I was lucky enough to land in Thailand in the booming sixties, but, as I like to remind my team, the harder we worked, the luckier we seemed to get.

Lucky breaks come in many different forms — the business opportunities that arise, the people you hire, the personal contacts you make, and the good health you enjoy. Looking back, I think one of my first really lucky breaks was not taking my father's advice to leave Thailand. Dad, who as a *Voice of America* correspondent, had an excellent grasp of world affairs, told me to try my luck in Iran or the Philippines. He thought Thailand would be a poor place in which to do business. That sounds crazy now, but in the late 1960s it appeared to be very sound advice. Under the Shah of Iran and Ferdinand Marcos, the economies of both Iran and the Philippines were expanding and stable. I had been raised in Asia, and the Philippines appeared to have a lot going for it. Economically, it was way ahead of Thailand and, because of the American defense force presence, there were many Western influences in mainstream society.

I would love to say that I saw the Thai boom coming through pure intuition and entrepreneurial brilliance. The truth is rather different. I didn't want to go to university back in the U.S., a place that held little attraction for me. I liked Thailand, I liked the people, I liked go-karting, I liked earning money. I liked my life. Thailand was FUN. My family had contacts in Bangkok — having parents on the diplomatic social circuit didn't hurt, and doors tended to swing open. So I stayed in Thailand, started my cleaning and advertising business, got married, and never looked back.

About seven years later, I was given another lucky break, probably the biggest of my working life. It materialized in rather odd circumstances. It was 1978 and the Vietnam War was over, as was the U.S. military's presence in Thailand. This was very bad news for many of the R&R establishments, which had entertained huge numbers of U.S. military personnel. Among these establishments was a little bungalow-style hotel in Pattaya that had fallen on hard times. I had always had a soft spot for the place as I had been there often when I was a kid, when the whole family often used to spend weekends by the sea.

The son of a wealthy Thai banking family let it be known that he held the rights to the lease and seemed very keen to step aside. My partner and I were sure we could make it work. It was to be my first venture into the hotel business and I was champing at the bit to get started. We opened negotiations and the deal was done. We deposited US$500,000 in the gentleman's bank account and he was to arrange for the lease to be transferred to the Bangkok Bank, the bank that had lent us the money, as security. As the land was owned by His Majesty the King's Private Property Office, the private investment arm of the royal family, we didn't give it a second thought. Well, the bank kept asking us where the lease was. I called up the King's Private Property Office and received a polite but shocking response. There was no lease available — it had expired some time ago because the rent was unpaid. We had been cheated. The man from the oh-so-respectable banking family had nothing to sell. It transpired that he had got himself into financial difficulties and was looking for someone to bail him out!

I was devastated. It seemed I had lost everything. I wasn't even 30 and my career as a hotel baron appeared to be over before it had even begun. We had borrowed millions of baht from the bank and had been sold a false promise. I was ruined. With nothing more to lose but my dignity, and there wasn't much of that left, I asked for an appointment to see the representative of the King's Private Property Office. As a *farang*, or foreigner, this was not very common and I was very surprised when I was granted a meeting.

I was ushered into a room and introduced to a gentleman by the name of M.L. Usni Pramoj. He asked me very politely what he could do for me. I explained the mess I was in and wondered if there was anything that could be done. His Majesty's representative looked at me and smiled. "Why didn't you ask us directly? There was no need to pay a fee for the rights to the lease. We would have given it to you for nothing providing you pay a fair amount every month."

My jaw hit the floor. We quickly worked out an arrangement to cover the back rent and negotiated a new lease of 100,000 baht a month (about US$4,000 in those days). The deal was done on the spot with a handshake. I dashed back to my office and immediately started legal proceedings against the man who had sold me the expired lease. I won, though it took 15 years.

What was important was that I was still in business and at the start of what turned out to be one of our most enduring business relationships. As I soon discovered, M.L. Usni wasn't only the son of a former prime minister, but was also a highly regarded advisor to His Majesty. It was the beginning of a long and trusting relationship with the King's Private Property Office.

We invested a lot of money in the Pattaya property, which eventually became the Pattaya Marriott Resort and Spa. We now pay a percentage of the sales rather than a flat rent, a business concept we pioneered in Thailand. The arrangement is of mutual benefit, as the better we do the larger the return for the landowners. We have done several hotel deals together with the King's personal property office and our relationship means we often don't have to buy land. Most of our hotels are built on percentage rents, a huge benefit when land can be so expensive that developers struggle to find the money to build the property.

Over the years, M.L. Usni and I became close friends and to this day our families wine, dine, holiday, and scuba dive together. Among many other things, I owe my love of fine wine to him. I have also had the honor of meeting His Majesty on a number of occasions, all of them memorable. More than anything else, it was His Majesty's dedication to Thailand, his great leadership, and his outstanding qualities that inspired me to become a Thai citizen.

Looking back, I have been blessed with a lot of good fortune. I believe that the opportunity I had to work for David Ogilvy when I was in the advertising business was another lucky break. I learnt a lot from him about how to run a company, and how to launch major campaigns and international accounts.

What you think is a setback can sometimes be a lucky break. For years, Burma (now called Myanmar) has been tipped as the next boom tourist market. It is a country that appears to have everything — an untouched coastline boasting beautiful beaches and unpolluted waters, and a rich history and heritage. Politically and economically, however, it remains a basket-case. I tried very hard to win the rights to build a hotel in Pagan, an ancient city that is the site of a magnificent temple complex. The Oriental beat me to it, and at the time

I cursed my bad luck. The hotel is still waiting to be built. In the capital, Rangoon, the Shangri-La outbid me for a plot of land. Suffice to say, the hotel the group built there hasn't been one of the Shangri-La's better investments. Sometimes the best deal is the one you *don't* clinch. I could have been sitting with an empty hotel in Rangoon for the last 10 years. It would have cost me millions, which would have been better spent on other more lucrative projects.

Good health is another great blessing. For a man who likes fast cars, motorcycles, flying, and scuba diving, I have led a charmed life and have hardly spilt a drop of my own blood nor broken a single bone. But I am no foolhardy daredevil. The secret of life in the fast lane is to obey the rules. There are old pilots and there are bold pilots, but there are no old, bold pilots. It doesn't matter if you are flying your own aircraft or racing a sports car at high speed, you must let your head make the decisions, not your heart. I always buy the best equipment and use the most experienced instructors. The key is to minimize the risks.

There is a parallel with gambling, here. I love to gamble at anything — dice, golf and, for me, nothing beats a good game of poker or blackjack. To me, gambling is, like business, a delicious mixture of luck, skill, making the most of opportunities, and taking responsibility for your own decisions. You have no-one to blame but yourself. If you misread the cards or your opponent, if you decide to take a card and bust, who are you going to blame? The dealer? The guy next to you? *You* made the decisions. If you lose all your money, *you* did it. If you doubled your money, *you* did it.

Yes, there is an element of luck involved, but any professional gambler will tell you that skill is the key to winning. It is the ability to count cards, to read your opponents, to know when to bluff and when to fold, that tips the scales in your favor. Good gamblers are always trying to minimize the risk, minimize the luck element, and make the most of the opportunities that come their way. Judging the odds in a game of cards is like assessing the risks of a business deal. I have taken a lot of chances in my life, but the odds were carefully calculated and, as a result, the risk was reduced. Professional gamblers win more often than they lose — just like successful entrepreneurs.

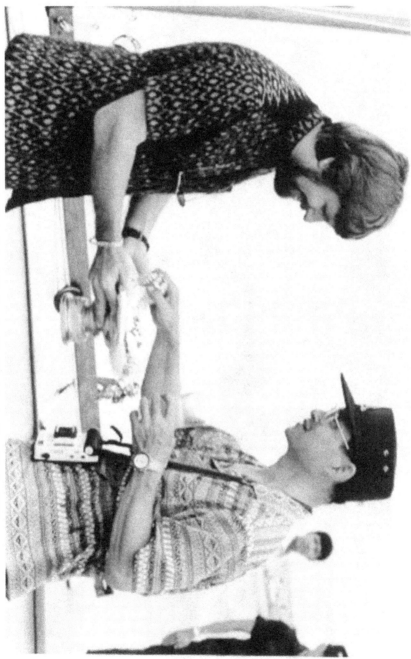

H.M. King Bhumibol of Thailand with Heinecke in Hua Hin in 1989

*The Managing Director of the Inter-Asian Enterprises and
Inter-Asian Publicity starting his career at age 18*

First hotel venture – The Royal Garden Resort, Pattaya. Today it is the Marriott Resort and Spa

The Regent Chiangmai, a Four Season Resort and Spa

With former U.K. Prime Minister, John Major in 1998
for the presentation of "Stars of Asia" BusinessWeek Award

With former U.S. President, George Bush at the
1999 CEO Forum in Hong Kong

PIZZA HUT PLANS TO DEVELOP AND RUN RESTAURANTS IN THAILAND SHOULD FRANCHISE CONTRACT END

Tricon Global Restaurants, Inc., parent company of Pizza Hut, announced contingency plans to build and operate new Pizza Hut restaurants in Thailand, should renewal negotiations with its franchisee, The Pizza Public Company Limited (PPCL) not be resolved. PPCL currently operates 116 Pizza Hut units in the Kingdom; however, the two companies have failed to reach an agreement to date on the renewal of the franchise contract which expires on 18 January, 2000.

"We are still hopeful we will come to terms with PPCL prior to the expiration of our current franchise agreement with them. However, if we are able to do so, we are fully prepared to develop and run the Pizza Hut brand ourselves", said Peter Hearl, Executive Vice President of Tricon Restaurants International. "Pizza Hut has become a well-established and very popular brand in Thailand, and we are commited to serving our customers "the best pizzas under one roof", in the Kingdom", Hearl said.

Tricon Global Restaurants, Inc. is the world's largest quick service restaurant company, with over 29,000 KFC, Pizza Hut and Taco Bell restaurants in over 100 countries. Worldwide system sales exceed US$20 Billion. In Thailand, in addition to the 116 Pizza Hut restaurants, the company also operates nearly 230 franchised and equity KFC units, employing about 4,500 associates in the Kingdom.

Tricon's full page ad that appeared in the Bangkok Post *and two other leading Thai newspapers*

Delivery Driver Conference on The Pizza Company Grand Opening Day,
March 17, 2001

An army of motorcyle delivery staff led by Bill Heinecke on the official
"D Day" of the launch of The Pizza Company, March 17, 2001

Taking down the "Pizza Hut" sign at the Royal Garden Plaza Thonburi,
1 of the 116 outlets closed on January 31, 2001

Thailand's Prime Minister Thaksin Shinawatra visiting The Pizza Company
outlet in Chiang Mai with his family

Learning to race Formula cars in France 1996

In a Robinson 22 after obtaining a helicopter license at the Civil Aviation Training Center in Hua Hin

Rule

13

Embrace Change As A Way Of Life

The graveyard of business is littered with companies that failed to recognize the need to change. — ***Anon***

The person who proposes change is going to have the most energy and the ideas, the best appreciation of what is needed to actually carry out the project. — ***Luciano Benetton***

M ost entrepreneurs are fairly flexible people. They are also open to new ideas and anticipate constant change. They have to. The past won't come around again, so neither isolation nor insulation from tomorrow is possible. The problems of the times are the opportunities of the future. Governments and new competitors, domestic and foreign, will increasingly affect the conduct of a given business, and so will social evolution. Vigilance is a great asset. The good entrepreneur always looks for new ways to do things and believes that, once it works, it will soon be obsolete. Change is constant. Change is everywhere. Deal with it, or your business will die.

I recently heard a lecture by Professor Jeremy Wiesen, from New York University's Stern School of Business, entitled "The Age of the Entrepreneur, 1980–99." Professor Wiesen made some fine points that are worth sharing here.

He reminded me how quickly the world has changed for entrepreneurs on so many different levels and how quickly we forget the speed of change. Here are just a few of the points he made:

On the computer: *Aside from the many sophisticated things that computers can do, there is basic word processing. I remember trying to do business plans in the early 1970s. The secretary would make a mistake, or I made a word or number change, and the whole page, or the whole plan if the change was long, had to be retyped. A few hours, or a day, later the document would come back from the secretary, usually requiring more changes and more delays and more frustration.*

On business ideology: *The 1970s were only 40 years from the beginning of the Great Depression and 25 years from the end of World War II. Optimists were a rare breed. When I tried to start a business in 1970, my parents thought I had gone mad. If you didn't work for others in an established company, you were an odd-ball to be avoided.*

On the Internet: *How could the giant bookstore retailer Barnes and Noble allow Amazon.com to gain such an enormous market share in full daylight? Big companies were asleep. Not only did they fail to initiate e-commerce, they watched it and still took five years to participate.*

On flexibility: *The success of start-up Internet-related companies is having an effect that goes beyond their impact on information technology and e-commerce. They have shown established companies that you cannot simply focus on a five-year plan set in stone which assumes that ways of doing business will not change drastically and that brand names and hundred-year-old relationships will remain powerful forever.*

As he spoke, I looked around the room and saw many people nodding their heads in agreement with almost everything he said.

Listen also to Bill Gates:

The entrepreneurial mindset continues to thrive at Microsoft because one of our major goals is to reinvent ourselves — we have to make sure that we are the ones replacing our products instead of someone else.[1]

Microsoft spends more than US$2 billion a year on research and redevelopment, because Bill Gates knows that every product the company sells will be obsolete within a few years.

I'm very glad that all businesses don't undergo such rapid change as at Microsoft, but the point about technology is well made. I chuckle when I think back to our early days. We used manual typewriters, and relied on carbon paper to make copies. (If we wanted to make ten copies of a contract, it could take a whole day!) We thought the telex machine a marvel of modern technology. I admit I was a slow learner when it came to technology. For years I followed the conventional wisdom that computers were changing so rapidly, there was no point in learning how to use one. For many years I didn't know how to use a computer and I didn't want to learn. If you take that approach, you are doomed. Of course, now I can't imagine doing business without PCs, CD-Roms, mobile phones, voicemail, and the Internet. I have just taught my 83-year-old mother how to use e-mail!

I am no cyberspace nerd, but I have realized that it's no use taking a lukewarm approach to new technology. Embrace it and hire the best people you can. We employ an outstanding individual to run our computer network who is paid a lot of money. She is worth her weight in gold, because she is always advising us on how the computer system can improve the business. Thanks to new technology, I can get a breakdown on almost any part of my business at the touch of a button. But it's important that all your staff keep up to speed. People who understand the possibilities that technology can bring to their areas of responsibility are the ones who adjust best to change. If the human resources department is doing its job, your staff will be receiving regular computer and information technology training. Once your company falls behind, it's very hard to catch up. Your rivals probably won't make the same mistake. No ambitious company, however small, can afford to ignore technology.

Change occurs on all fronts. Today's business environment is a highly complex one. Stock-market regulations, audit committees, securities commissions, financial instruments, potential conflicts of interest — the list goes on. Business practices, too, have moved on dramatically. For example, we share a great deal of information with our staff these days, including monthly and annual profit targets, turnover, and a lot more data that used to be highly confidential. Our corporate policy is now generally one of inclusion.

But if technology and business methods have been transformed, they are perhaps only a reflection of the waves of change that have washed across Asia on many fronts. When I started my business, the Americans were fighting in Vietnam and using military bases in Thailand to launch bombing raids on the north. China was a closed country experiencing the horrors of the Cultural Revolution. Taiwan, the Philippines, and South Korea were military dictatorships; and the economies of Singapore and Malaysia had yet to start their remarkable period of growth. Hong Kong has survived and prospered by reinventing itself from a cheap manufacturing base into a financial service center and business hub for southern China. Everywhere you look, whole industries have become obsolete, other markets have evolved, and people's aspirations have undergone radical changes. Indeed, if you had suggested 25 years ago that the whole region — the whole world, in fact — would change as dramatically as it has in the last quarter-century, you would have very likely been dismissed as a fool.

However, change doesn't have to be momentous for it to be important to the entrepreneur. The fall of the Berlin Wall in 1989 will be recorded in the history books as a defining moment in Europe. The fact that the sausage seller on the eastern side of the city could suddenly expand his operation into a wealthier market and make a decent profit will not.

For entrepreneurs, a simple innovation can be the start of something important. For example, when I opened my first Pizza Hut, it was a great success, so it was a sound business move to open a second, third, and fourth outlet. But what should our next step be? What would give us the edge and a guaranteed increased cash flow and market share at a time when the competition was moving in on our territory? We introduced home delivery. This was a huge change for Bangkok and for our business. Even in 1989, no-one else had tried it here. The main reason was the traffic problem: it was so awful, how could home delivery of *anything* work? The food would be stone-cold by the time it arrived, and cold pizza has never been a great promotional marketing tool.

Pizza Hut had been delivering to homes across the United States for years. There, the driver used his own car and was paid so much per trip. Problem number 2: in Thailand, delivery boys don't have cars. The solution was staring us in the face. One of the big changes that had taken place in Thailand in the 1960s and 1970s was the huge level of investment in the country by the Japanese. This injected a lot of jobs and money into the economy. One by-product was that the streets of Bangkok were teeming with small Japanese motorcycles.

Anyone who has been to Bangkok will know that the only way you can guarantee to beat the traffic is to take a motorcycle taxi. The journey may be one of the most hair-raising you are ever likely to experience (always remember to keep your knees tucked in), but you won't be late for that important appointment. But how were we going to make sure our delivery team was reliable, especially in the early days when the public was trying out our new service? We devised a scheme that would make it highly attractive for people to work for us.

We would make the down-payment on the motorcycle, which meant that we owned it. Then we said to the delivery guy: "You are going to pay us the balance out of your commission and salary over the next two years. You can ride it whenever you like, and after two years it's yours to keep." It was a win–win situation. He got the motorcycle with no down-payment, but he had to maintain it. We knew he was going to look after it, because it was in his interest to do so. This way, we didn't have the burden of looking after a thousand motorcycles, but we had a huge delivery fleet. The plan worked like a dream. Bangkok took to home delivery with as much enthusiasm as our delivery team took to the motorcycle scheme. Business boomed and other people soon copied us. Today, 1,200 Pizza Company employees deliver to more than 1.4 million households every year.

After that, we introduced a one-telephone-number ordering service for all our Pizza Hut operations. Again, this system was in use all over the United States, but not in Thailand. It was a huge success, and everyone else started to follow in our footsteps. I was interviewed in early 1999 by a reporter from the *Bangkok Post* who was writing a story about the expansion of Pizza Hut in Thailand. As an experiment, I asked him what our one-number delivery telephone number was. "712 7000" came the instant reply. At the time, it was the best-known telephone number in Thailand. We had to change it to 1112 when we launched The Pizza Company after the legal dispute with Tricon over Pizza Hut. This number has really caught on too and has played an important role in making the new brand a huge success. It was one of the first 4-digit nationwide "delivery" numbers.

So, out of social change came opportunity, and we grasped it with both hands. The experience confirmed my theory that people are basically the same everywhere and that most concepts that work in the West will work in Asia, although timing is always critical. A small but significant innovation helped to make us the biggest restaurant chain in Thailand, which led to our being listed on the stock exchange.

But what is the next market or trend, and where is the next happy hunting ground for the hungry entrepreneur? I have been keeping my eye on Vietnam for years. I was working in Bangkok when people were convinced Thailand would be consumed by the Communists after the fall of Saigon in 1975. I watched Vietnam close its doors to the West and had a front-row seat as it struggled to stand on its own two feet. By 1993, the per capita GNP was a pitiful US$200 a year, making it one of the poorest countries in the world. When President Clinton lifted the U.S. trade embargo in 1994, many people were tipping Vietnam as the next boom country in Southeast Asia.

After my experience of trying to get into the vending machine market too early, I watched and waited ... and waited ... and waited. Every time there was good news about the Vietnamese economy, it was matched by some gloomy press report about excessive red tape and corruption. A lot of smart people got badly burnt by rushing in before they knew enough about local conditions.

I was keen to be a player, but I didn't want us to have a lot of exposure in what was still a difficult market. We decided to hedge our bets. As tourism was one area that was expanding every year, I was keen not to miss the boat. On the other hand, I was wary about opening a hotel in Ho Chi Minh City, which seemed to have more than enough accommodation for visitors. We decided to dip our toe into the market by building a business hotel amid ten-story office towers in the port city of Haiphong, Vietnam's third-largest city. It opened in 1998, targeting both business people drawn to the rebuilt port area and tourists who wanted to visit the area's untouched beaches and the beauty of Halong Bay to the north.

It was a disaster from day one. The Haiphong Harbour View Hotel opened just after the financial crisis swept through Asia in 1997. Room rates were only US$35 and occupancy was 25%. We dropped the rate to US$25 and occupancy fell even further. The idea was that the hotel would attract all the businessmen visiting the two industrial estates built by the government and foreign partners. Even today, the estates are still empty. We are getting some trade from tourists stopping off on their way to Ha Long Bay and a few desperate punters visiting Stanley Ho's casino at nearby Do San. I have a feeling that Mr Ho — Macau's wealthiest man and a very smart businessman — shares my lack of enthusiasm for investing in north Vietnam at the moment!

By 2002, the hotel was just starting to break even. It is going to take a total of 17 years to pay the banks back the money we borrowed. The lesson here is, don't start projects in places you are not particularly keen on. As soon as something goes wrong you are going to be spending a lot of time there. That's why I got out of the pizza business in Beijing in the early 1990s (although I must admit we are looking carefully at the possibility of taking The Pizza Company there now). I would have got out of Haiphong years ago, but no one wanted to buy the hotel. Perhaps staying in Vietnam will eventually be another blessing in disguise!

The jury may still be out on Vietnam, but our idea was to test the waters with a small investment and to network like crazy so that we would be ready to move into restaurants and food when the time was right. The point I wish to make here is that change comprises the constant ebb and flow of small occurrences, as well as the dramatic events that make headlines and end up in the history books. Many of the small changes in Vietnam are the knock-on effects of the major upheavals, such as the lifting of the trade embargo and the impact of the recent Asian crisis. You have to try to keep on top of them all. It is important to read both the mainstream newspapers and the trade press. *The Economist* might publish a brilliant analysis of the changes taking place in Vietnam's banking laws, but only a specialist food magazine will tell you how to buy a pizza oven in Hanoi. Both are very different pieces of news, but they can be equally important to the entrepreneur.

How best to cope with change is not in itself a new concept. As Henry Ford long ago observed:

Habit conduces to a certain inertia. Businessmen go down with their businesses because they like the old way so well they cannot bring themselves to change. One sees them all about — men who do not know that yesterday is past and who woke up this morning with last year's ideas. It could almost be written down as a formula that when a man begins to think that he has at last found his method he had better begin a most searching examination of himself to see whether some part of his brain has not gone to sleep. There is a subtle danger in a man thinking that he is "fixed" for life. It indicates that the next jolt of the wheel of progress is going to fling him off.[2]

I am determined never to make that mistake. I wanted to prove to myself that I could learn something new and complex before I turned 50, so I learnt how to fly a helicopter. To paraphrase Henry Ford, if you are an old dog and you don't keep yourself young enough to learn new tricks, you're finished.

Notes

1. Janet Lowe, *Bill Gates Speaks* (John Wiley & Sons, New York, 1998).
2. Peter Krass (ed.), *The Book of Business Wisdom* (John Wiley & Sons, New York, 1997), p. 342.

Rule

14

Develop Your Contacts

When you meet someone who inspires you, ask for their help.

— Anon

A successful entrepreneur must cultivate his or her business and social contacts. No-one can be successful in a vacuum. The entrepreneur needs to establish an extensive network of bankers, lawyers, advisors, accountants, analysts, investors, politicians, journalists, and, most importantly, customers. Goodwill is always essential and cannot be bought; it must be earned. Nurturing and cultivating contacts is like growing a tree — if it's done successfully, the branches keep spreading and one is connected to another. It is fundamental to your success, especially in Asia, where the business relationship often comes before the economic fundamentals.

When I was just starting out, I would work all day and entertain five nights a week. I never missed an opportunity to remind our bankers that my company represented a safe haven for their loans. These days, I have an extensive network of contacts in place, and I prefer to cement those relationships at my own pace.

I still encourage my key executives to network energetically and intelligently. Too many executives meet too many of their own kind. This is very one-dimensional, and the weakness of such a strategy will show up in the long term.

For me, one of the all-time great networkers is Kurt Wachtveitl, the manager of the Oriental in Bangkok, the world's finest hotel. Kurt is always hosting cocktail and dinner parties, always developing his relationships with customers and potential customers, political, business, and financial movers and shakers, and his competitors. I will declare an interest here. Kurt and I have known each other for more than 30 years. When I first knew him, he was the manager of a more humble hotel, the Nipa Lodge, in Pattaya. In 1968, his last act in charge of that establishment was to give me and my new bride Kathy free accommodation as a wedding present.

Shortly afterwards, he took up the position of general manager of the Oriental and has been there ever since. His contacts book must be the envy of everyone in the hotel business.

Another Asian networker extraordinaire is my financier friend Anil Thadani, who has invested in many of my projects over the years. Anil has worked in San Francisco, Tokyo, Manila and Hong Kong. In all, he has helped invest more than US$1.5 billion in 70 deals in 12 countries. One of his most famous successes was to co-found Amanresorts with Adrian Zecha. These ultra-luxurious resorts are today the playgrounds of the rich and famous, and one of the few businesses founded in Asia to have reached a position of undisputed global leadership in its field.

Successful entrepreneurs must get to know the opposition. If you get to know your competitors, you soon discover who the star performers are and set about the business of poaching them. The woman who runs our marketing department at Swensen's was previously marketing director of Dominos. We thought she was doing a brilliant job for them, so we hired her at the first opportunity. If you don't get out and meet the people who are beating you to the punch, you'll never know where you are going wrong.

Be aware that you don't have exclusive rights to great ideas and brilliant people. Make a mental or written note of the people who impress you, or who are doing a great job. When the time comes to expand your team or fill a vacancy, you should always be in a position to know who would make a great addition to your company. Like a good boy scout, be prepared. Anyone can quit suddenly or be knocked down by a bus, so you must always be ready to replace people quickly.

When we bought 25% of the Regent Hotel in Bangkok, the fact that we knew the board members and the hotel operators was probably more important to us than checking their books. It wasn't regarded as a hostile purchase. Their managers weren't afraid of us — they liked us, and we liked them. The chairman of the Regent Hotel, my friend M.L. Usni Pramoj, encouraged me to try to buy this important stake to ensure that the hotel remained in Thai hands. The relationship made a critical difference in assisting the deal to go through smoothly.

In the early stages of your career, it is very important to expand your contacts. It's part of the art of selling yourself. But making contacts doesn't just mean exchanging name cards and shaking hands. It means picking the right contacts and developing the important relationships. Be selective; you can't have lunch with everyone you meet. Out of 20 cards you might collect at a business function, only three might belong to people who are interesting or potentially useful in some way. Take great care in choosing the people in whom you are prepared to invest time.

Likewise, once you have access to important people, don't waste their time. I could probably reach several Thai cabinet ministers on the phone if I really had to, but I would only do so if the matter at hand was important enough to justify taking up their time. Don't abuse the relationship by calling important contacts for small favors. If you do, you will soon discover that the person is unavailable next time you call.

In 1978, I became the youngest president of the American Chamber of Commerce in Thailand. I was only 27, and it gave me a real kick because the same organization had refused my first application to join in 1968 because at that time, at age 18, I was considered too young. Back then, Amcham was a rather stuffy, conservative, staid organization. At our regular monthly meetings, we really believed we knew what was going on in

Thailand. The members were almost completely insulated from the outside world, because we were listening to each other and had no input from influential Thais. We Americans were feeding ourselves disinformation without knowing it. I was determined to introduce change when I became president and suggested we invite some Thai directors on to the board. We actually had to change the rules so that certain directors could be appointed and not face the rigors (and potential embarrassment) of an election. We could hardly invite senior members of Thai society to join the chamber and then tell them they had to be voted into office.

The first three Thai gentlemen we invited were Anand Panyarachun, Amaret Sila-On, and Tarrin Nimmanahaeminda. I think it is safe to say they were wise selections. Anand went on to become one of Thailand's great prime ministers. In 1991, the Thai government was toppled in a coup and Anand was persuaded by His Majesty the King to accept the post of interim prime minister until fresh elections were held. His ability to lead and his reputation for integrity made him a popular figure, and he was invited back as a caretaker prime minister in 1992 after the country experienced more violence. It is generally agreed that Anand's steady hand helped to strengthen the democratic process and to guide Thailand away from the influence of the military. We are still good friends today, and he paid me the honour of officially opening the JW Marriott Phuket Resort and Spa in 2001.

Amaret is a former minister of commerce and was appointed chairman of the Financial Sector Restructuring Authority (FRA), another important body given the responsibility of helping to clean up the financial mess of the late 1990s. Tarrin became president of the Siam Commercial Bank, Thailand's oldest bank, before becoming the finance minister charged with digging Thailand out of the Asian crisis of 1997.

Back in 1978, these three men already had great insight into what was *really* happening in their country, and their input allowed the chamber to hear for the first time what well-connected, influential Thais were thinking. This innovation made me a more successful president of Amcham and hasn't exactly hurt me in business. It has allowed me to pick up the phone and reach the most senior bankers in the country, especially in times of crisis like 1997. You have to remember that for many years, like all foreigners, I was considered an outsider in Thai business circles, so it was extremely important for me to break down barriers, establish solid relationships, and try to become accepted.

Looking back, there were several distinct phases in this process. After the survival phase and a period of consolidation, people started to take us seriously. It was then possible to start building relationships with influential Thai families. In the old days, it was said that there were 16 extended families who ran the 16 banks. Much later, we found that some American multinationals were seeking us out. They didn't need us for our money; they wanted our connections and relationships, and our knowledge of how to do business successfully in Thailand.

It is important to establish a reputation as someone who doesn't use people for short-term gains. It took me almost ten years before my credibility was of sufficient standing to enter into partnership with two prominent Thai families — the powerful industrialist Narongdej's family and the Chirathivat family, owners of the Central retail group. Having excellent references never hurt anyone.

You can make great contacts in the strangest circumstances. As I mentioned earlier, my first meeting with

M.L. Usni Pramoj, the representative of His Majesty the King's Private Property Office, occurred when I was on the verge of losing my very first hotel deal. He helped me sort out the mess, and that was the start of one of my most enduring business friendships.

The successful entrepreneur also knows how to attract favorable attention, both inside his field and, more broadly, in the media. One well-publicized success will cover up a multitude of blunders. Good media contacts can help you to celebrate your successes.

Public relations companies are good up to a point, but nothing beats personal contacts. Someone once called me and asked how I managed to get our company results into the *Asian Wall Street Journal* so quickly. Easy. I picked up the phone and called the correspondent, whom I knew, and then faxed him the information. It was newsworthy information — our industry is often a key economic indicator — and the story ran in the newspaper the next day. The journalist knew that I wouldn't call him unless I had something of real interest to tell him.

We try to keep on good terms with the press. By developing good relationships with selected journalists, we can have off-the-record conversations when we need to. I recommend that you try to get to know the editor of the biggest newspaper in town. They are normally very keen to do a lot of networking themselves and usually spend time on the social circuit.

The importance of having a good relationship with the media was illustrated during our lengthy tussle with Goldman Sachs for the Regent Bangkok in 1999 (see Rule 20). Not only were we able to put our side of the story in a wide range of publications but, more often than not, we were portrayed as the Thai David facing up to Goldman, the U.S. Goliath. To say the least, that did us no harm at all.

It's also smart to be quite choosy about the publications in which you appear. Aim high and don't appear to be too accessible. When we opened the Regent Chiang Mai, we didn't have a huge budget with which to advertise internationally. Instead, we used our media network and an excellent public relations officer, Lee Sutton. Prestigious U.S. magazines such as *Town & Country, Travel and Leisure,* and *Architectural Digest* all ran very complimentary pieces. Most of our early guests came on the strength of those articles. Later, during the legal battle with Tricon over Pizza Hut, we hired a public relations firm called DMG. It was essential that we got our side of the story over to the media, and the press lapped it up. DMG did a great job of spreading the message that Tricon were the bad guys in this story — a giant U.S. corporation determined to crush the Thai underdog by any means. There is no doubt that we won the PR war against Tricon, and this helped The Pizza Company become a great success story after we lost the Pizza Hut franchise.

It is also a sound strategy to emerge as a spokesperson for your industry. These days, I am often asked to comment on developments in the fast-food or hotel industries. When we make a presentation to analysts, we take a leadership role — we tell them what is happening with our company as well as the industry, so we appear to be the market leaders even if we're not. What is important is that we use the opportunity to behave like the market leader.

Some companies shun the media completely. I think this is unwise. While I don't believe in the old adage that there is no such thing as bad publicity, good press contacts can make all the difference.

Rule

15

Use Your Time Wisely

Everyone has the same 24 hours in a day; it is what you do with them that counts. — ***Anon***

The single most important resource that we allocate from one moment to the next is our own time. How you handle your own time is, in my view, the single most important aspect of being a role model. — ***Andrew S. Grove***

Time is limited, and time, to an entrepreneur, is money. Most of the way we use our time is habitual, and we don't know how we spend our time until we try to keep track of it. It's amazing how easy it is to waste this precious commodity without really noticing. It just slips away.

How does a project get to be a month behind? The answer is simple: one day at a time. Great discipline is needed to extract the most out of each day, week, weekend, and month. A good routine is a sound place to start, as this can help you to identify areas of waste. Other things to consider are your support team, how to get the most out of meetings, how to deal with paperwork, and how to use your time outside the office to your best advantage.

Let's start with routine. I rise at 7 a.m., shower and eat some fruit for breakfast. My driver arrives to pick me up at 7.45 a.m. By the time I reach the office 30 minutes later I have scanned the *Asian Wall Street Journal* and two local newspapers. I feel out of the loop if I don't know what's happening in Thailand, Asia, and the world by the time I'm behind my desk. Wall Street, U.S. interest rates, the value of the baht, and business and political developments are all fundamental to my business. I also read the *Far Eastern Economic Review, Time,* and numerous trade publications.

The first job of the day is to prepare a list of all the people I need to talk to on the telephone. The order depends on time zones in different parts of the world and the relative importance of the call. As I make up to 50 calls a day my staff have become expert at getting the right people on the line at the right time. In the course of a day, I'll touch base with all our businesses — fast food, hotels, marketing, and manufacturing. I try to speak to all my key executives once a day. I also receive daily sales returns from all our hotels as well as more than 300 restaurants and 100 retail outlets. All the information is online, which saves a huge amount of time. E-mail allows me to communicate with all our top executives daily anytime in the country or the world. I send and receive up to a hundred e-mails a day.

I nearly always take lunch in the office. There are two reasons for this: these days I can normally get people to come to me, and the traffic can be so awful that a lunch-time appointment can wipe out several afternoon appointments.

I work till 7.30 p.m. or later, then go home and have dinner with Kathy. I use the time in the car to finish whatever I failed to complete in the office. My schedule is nothing like as grueling as it used to be in the early days, and I attend far fewer business dinners than I used to. It's worth remembering that exhausted, brain-dead executives don't perform very well.

I do an enormous amount of work by dictaphone. My first executive secretary presented me with one years ago and told me I would be much more productive if I didn't make her take dictation in shorthand and then type it up and waste time for both of us. She was right; now I dictate all notes and letters wherever I happen to be — in the office, the car, a plane, or the bathtub. E-mail allows me to respond personally to queries from our executives and even our customers.

I rely heavily on a support team of two executive secretaries, a personal assistant, and my driver. David Ogilvy trained me to take copious notes, so I am forever giving staff members pieces of paper. I am also a list person. I make daily lists, weekly lists, and monthly lists. I get a real kick out of making a list in the morning and being able to check off the items dealt with during the course of the day. Then I start a list for the next day. Never underestimate the effectiveness of making lists.

Someone once wrote that secretaries are the most misused resource in business. They were right. The traditional image of someone who makes tea and performs a few other menial tasks is sadly outdated. New technology has opened the door to a new era in which secretaries can play key roles in the business. My team is often the first to hear important news about sales figures or the decision to buy a hotel. I would be lost without them, as they organize every moment of my time. They have been with me for a long time and I think that, together, we make a very good team.

The two areas that suck more time out of your day than anything else are meetings and paperwork. Try to keep meetings short and to the point. Have an agenda and stick to it. If people start to go off at tangents, stop them quickly even if you have to be a little rude. I like what Bill Gates has to say on the subject:

> *When I go to a meeting, I keep specific objectives in mind. There isn't much small talk, especially if I'm with colleagues I know well. We discuss accounts we lost or where overhead is too high, and then we are done. Bang! There are always more challenges than there are hours, so why be wasteful?*[1]

Jorma Ollila, CEO of Nokia, put it this way:

> *Time is the key issue. I hate meetings and pointless memo writing. Meetings do not get things done, people do.*[2]

Who could disagree?

It's the same with paperwork — lose control of it and it will overwhelm you. Paperwork doesn't go away just because you say you don't have time to deal with it. It will sit there patiently and grow as more reports and memos pile up. I admire the approach taken by J.W. Marriott, Jr., chairman and CEO of Marriott International Inc., with whom we do a lot of hotel business. His secret is to handle each piece of paper that comes across his desk once only.

> *As promised by time management gurus, this small act of self-discipline has amazing effects, he says. Not only does it keep the avalanche of paper that comes into my office somewhat under control, the daily practice keeps me in training for decision-making on a larger scale.*[3]

I can't swear that I always succeed in following his advice, but I do try my best. I often put papers in a pending tray if I don't feel the need to deal with them immediately. It's amazing, but half of those matters will have resolved themselves by the time I go back and look through the tray. I just deal with the rest.

Another area where I think business people can use their time more productively is when they are on overseas trips. Many regard plane journeys as dead time, but if you follow some fairly simple rules, your time in the air can be useful. First of all, travel light. You'll save yourself up to an hour at either end if you don't have to wait around for your baggage. If you pack sensibly, you can almost always squeeze everything you need into a carry-on bag.

Once on the plane, never talk to your neighbors. I know this sounds unsociable, but you will find that once that first conversation has taken place you could be interrupted while you are preparing yourself for important negotiations on arrival. Look on the bright side: this approach could also save you from being on the wrong end of some very boring stories.

Also, be wary of the drinks trolley. Alcohol seems to speed through the bloodstream far faster in a pressurized cabin; even a beer followed by a glass or two of wine over dinner can impair your powers of concentration when you are trying to write that killer speech or finalize your sales pitch. Wait until you get to the hotel and treat yourself to a nightcap. One last travel tip: if you make frequent trips to a city, always stay in the same hotel. It will save you time and a lot of hassles.

I think too many business people waste time on tasks to which they're ill-suited. Entrepreneurs are generally people with strengths in certain areas, so it makes no sense to dedicate many hours to areas in which they are weak. Do the things *you* do best, and have others do the rest. If you are delegating wisely, you will save yourself valuable time and produce better results. Use the talents that have got you where you are. If finance isn't your strong suit but selling is, then spend your time selling and hire the best financial brains to work the bottom line.

How successful you are as an entrepreneur will depend on how well you exploit your strengths, not on how much you have improved on your weaknesses. Half of being smart is knowing what you are dumb at. I am better at presenting a speech than writing it, so I use the best speechwriter I can, who usually happens to be my brother, Skip. He can write much better speeches than I can in half the time. Remember, everyone has the same 24 hours in a day; it's what you do with them that counts.

Here are some golden rules that can help you save time:

- Keep a time log so that you can identify and eliminate unproductive habits.
- Schedule your most important tasks for prime time, the time of day when you work at your best.

- Before you tackle a job, ask yourself: "Is this the best use of my time and energy?" If the answer is "no," get someone else to do the job or don't do it.
- Don't get strangled by paperwork. Never ask for something on paper unless it is absolutely necessary.
- Learn how to use a dictaphone. You will find it will save you valuable time.
- Spend the last few minutes of each day preparing a list of tasks for the next day.
- Make use of the word "no." Don't burden yourself with an impossible workload.
- Slice a large, unpleasant task into many small tasks. The key is to make each job simple and quick. This is called the "salami" technique.
- Interruptions can't be eliminated entirely, but try to keep them to a minimum. An hour of concentrated effort is worth more than two hours of broken thought.
- Delegate tasks whenever possible, but make sure you give people the authority to get the job done.
- Don't accumulate a backlog of half-completed business. Once you start a job, finish it.

Manage your time before it flies away. Remember, it never comes back.

Notes

[1] Janet Lowe, *Bill Gates Speaks* (John Wiley & Sons, New York, 1998).

[2] The Performance Group, *The Keys to Breakthrough Performance* (Bjelland, Dahl and Partners, New York), p. 67.

[3] J.W. Marriott, *The Spirit to Serve, Marriot's Way* (HarperBusiness, New York, 1997).

Rule

16

Measure For Measure

There are only two qualities in the world: efficiency and inefficiency, and only two sorts of people: the efficient and the inefficient.
— **George Bernard Shaw**

It is an immutable law in business that words are words, explanations are explanations, and promises are promises, but only performance is reality.   — **Anon**

When you can measure what you are speaking about and express it in numbers, you know something about it; but when you cannot measure it, when you cannot express it in numbers, your knowledge is of a meager and unsatisfactory kind.   — **William Kelvin**

B enchmarking has become one of today's corporate buzz words. The expression is such a newcomer to the business scene that my dictionary defines a benchmark by its original meaning: — "a mark cut in rock by surveyors." So, what exactly is benchmarking? I suppose the most widely accepted definition is the identification and adoption of best practices or techniques for performing common tasks, assessing job performance, and setting performance goals. This involves looking at the methods used by your own organization, by recognized market leaders, and by your direct competitors.

Originally used by the computer industry to compare the processing power of competing products, the term "benchmarking" moved into the mainstream when Xerox first made use of it in 1979. By 1981, Xerox had embraced benchmarking wholeheartedly after coming under intense pressure from its Japanese competitors. The company's executives sat down and asked themselves the following ten simple questions:

1. What is the most critical factor to my organization's success?
2. What factors are causing the most trouble?
3. What products or services are provided to customers?
4. What factors account for customer satisfaction?
5. What specific problems have been identified in the organization?
6. Where are the competitive pressures being felt in the organization?
7. What are the major costs in the organization?
8. Which functions represent the highest percentage of cost?
9. Which functions have the greatest room for improvement?

10. Which functions differentiate the organization from its competitors?[1]

Word of Xerox's innovation spread quickly in the corporate world and U.S. giants AT & T, Motorola, and Westinghouse soon followed suit. Now there is a substantial global benchmarking industry, complete with countless websites and armies of consultants. A recent Internet search turned up 20,000 entries!

Benchmarking is the cornerstone of continuous improvement. It makes you focus on basic issues such as how you can improve and how others are doing the same thing better. A good manager should always have a healthy disregard for the status quo. Benchmarking allows this dissatisfaction to be channeled into productive change.

For us, the fact that we want to measure ourselves and see how we compare against the best is a sign that our business has matured. Entrepreneurs find it difficult to benchmark early on, because they are too busy trying to stay on their feet. Benchmarking suits established businesses.

We try to measure everybody and everything — hotels, restaurants, janitors, drivers, bell boys, chief executives — you name it. The minute you start measuring people, you can start driving their performance. Imagine, with a staff of 12,000, if you could get every single person on the payroll to improve their performance by 10%. The difference to the group would be enormous. Remember, we are one of the few big employers in Thailand that isn't unionized. We want to motivate people, to challenge them to improve, improvise, innovate, and think outside the box. Our success depends on many people now; it is no longer a question of how well *I* am performing.

We want each member of our staff to measure themselves against their peers and rivals. The same goes for each department, each hotel, each restaurant, and each company. It's a question of seeing who has the best practices and trying to match them. Once you have achieved that, you can try to exceed them.

Take the Oriental Hotel, for example. I tell all our hotel staff that it is the world's best hotel and challenge them to compete against it step by step, day by day, by trying to supply better value for money. We charge US$100 for a basic room at the Bangkok Marriott Resort and Spa, which is ten minutes down the river from the Oriental which charges US$300. Is the experience three times better than at our hotel? If it is not, then we are doing a good job. If their standards are seen to be only 20% better than ours, then we are providing fabulous value for the average traveler. But you can only compare like with like, and the Oriental, of course, has that one quality that cannot be bought — its history. It is still easy to close your eyes and imagine Somerset Maugham sitting out on the terrace watching the world go by on the river.

Just across the river, a worthy challenger to the Oriental is emerging. When the Peninsula opened in Bangkok in 1998, I sent my managers out on scouting missions. They returned looking just a little smug. They said the service was a tad slow and the prices were outrageous. I went up the river to do a little benchmarking of my own and came back with a rather different impression. I was blown away by the quality, the attention to detail, and the overall excellence. I warned my managers that it doesn't take long to get the service up to speed in a new hotel. I also reminded them that our service was a little slow when we first opened. I told them that I believed the Peninsula would become the best hotel in

Thailand in a few years. Whether the owners make any money is another matter. It is said they spent US$1 million on each room! And I believe it. Their rooms are the most sophisticated, electronically, I have ever seen. The quality of the materials used throughout is astonishing. I know, down to the finest detail, what goes into building a hotel and I marvel at what they have achieved. It is also interesting to note that the Peninsula is on the same, "wrong", side of the river as our own Bangkok Marriott Resort and Spa. Interestingly the Peninsula was named the number 1 hotel in Thailand and the number 2 in the world by *Travel and Leisure* Magazine in 2002.

So, benchmarking should be a state of mind rather than a performance review. A good employee should always be asking himself or herself: "How can I do my job better?" The process never stops, and for me it is a personal passion as well as a corporate philosophy. Whenever I visit a restaurant or a hotel, I am always looking around, comparing, and measuring. I check out the menus, the prices in the business center — anything that I can compare with our own products and services. When I was last in Singapore I stayed at the Ritz Carlton and I noticed they had introduced a breakfast menu in Japanese. What a good idea — the Japanese market is a significant one in Singapore. They had also introduced a range of special services for the suites, which offered very large bathtubs, bubble bath, a bottle of champagne, and a wonderful view over Singapore harbor — what more could two lovebirds want? I store all this information away for future reference.

Benchmarking is all about details. We ask all our guests to fill in questionnaires. The people who return the forms are either very happy or very unhappy, so you always learn something. We often find that people from the United States and Europe are bowled over by the level of service. The Bangkok Marriott Resort and Spa has been rated the top Marriott in the Asia-Pacific region, and number 2 worldwide. I attribute this to our successful benchmarking. We arrange for "mystery customers," selected by an independent company, to visit our restaurants, such as Benihana's, the Japanese-American steakhouse, to check on the service and presentation. The "customer" might, say, deliberately knock over a cup of coffee and then make a report on what happened. Did the waiter bring a fresh cup, or just take the old one away? Or he might change his order, to see what the response was. Did the waiter say, "No problem, Sir," or tell the customer: "This is what you ordered." How do the staff handle difficult problems, especially when they are busy? How are the customers greeted? We aim for 100% customer satisfaction, so nothing but the best is tolerated.

Our employees are part of the benchmarking process. We are measuring their performance, so they must be able to measure their own contribution. In the old days, we shared very little information with our staff. It was confidential data circulated only to senior executives on a need-to-know basis. These days, the opposite is true. Unlike so many companies in Asia, we no longer pay an annual bonus. In 1997, we couldn't pay a bonus because we were fighting for our financial lives. In 1998, we told everyone that if we made money, a bonus of one month's salary would be paid, but it would be the last time. Annual bonuses had become a right, not a privilege. Staff simply expected them to be paid, regardless of their performance. We felt it was time to change our business practices and to challenge the staff to measure their performance and benefits at the same time. In 1999, we told every member of staff what the monthly target figures were for their unit or company. "Every month you hit those targets, you will receive one-twelfth of your bonus — or 8.3% of your annual salary — in your monthly pay packet." The message was simple: if the company wins, you win, too. Now all staff members see the numbers almost as soon as we do. The experiment has been very successful.

Many people in the hotel business become too focused on average room rates and occupancy rates. These are useful benchmarks, but they can be misleading. For example, an average room rate of US$200 may look splendid on paper, but what if the hotel is only 10% occupied? It is the average yield per room — the amount of money each room makes — that is bankable.

However, benchmarking shouldn't become purely an obsession with numbers. All our hotels now conduct regular employee opinion surveys. This is a practice we adopted from Marriott, and it gives great insight into what the staff think about us. You also need managers who look at all aspects of the business, not just the bottom line. The sort of skill that is needed for all-round success is the ability to recruit a hotel staff of hundreds who can work together as a team and keep morale high. Our managers are now judged on a balanced scorecard. Part of their bonus is based on how their employees view them, customer satisfaction, as well as profit performance. This ensures that they do a good all-round job. It is easy to show a profit in a hotel if you don't replace the linen or the towels and cut back on maintenance and staff. Some expatriate "experts" in Asia on two-year contracts have been known to produce great profits but leave the hotel with no customers, because no-one wants to come back.

All our Marriott-branded hotels in Thailand are benchmarked against the showpiece Bangkok Marriott Resort and Spa, probably the best Marriott hotel in the world. Staff from Hua Hin and Pattaya visit regularly to see the operation first hand. How does the front desk greet guests? How efficient are the porters? What is the average response time for room service? The measuring process never stops. We also send all our managers to stay at the Oriental, the Peninsula, and the Regent. They have to experience what the best hotels feel like — the nuances, and the attention to detail. You can't learn about your opposition by just walking through their lobby. To benchmark properly, you have to be well past the survival stage and not worried about paying tomorrow's payroll. You have to spend money to grow to the next level. I want to run the premier hotel group in Thailand, and I want my staff to have the same vision.

We are constantly renovating our hotels. In the old days, we were lucky if we were looking ahead three months. Now we replace the elevators, the telephone systems, and the airconditioning as they become obsolete and better models come on the market. Consider this benchmark: Marriott has a renovation system for its hotels that allows the company to think up to ten years ahead! We still have a long way to go.

One of the ways we have developed is through being exposed to world-class companies and looking at their ideas and those of people we admire. For example, I admire Jack Welch at General Electric for creating core values and making people want to be part of the company. Marriott, Four Seasons and Dairy Queen are fine companies that continually help us with the latest technology and experience, which helps us to evaluate our own business practices regularly.

Gone are the days when I could go around every part of the operation and check things myself — there simply isn't the time. That isn't to say I won't fire off a memo whenever I see something I don't like. But there are limits to how much you can micro-manage when your business grows. While the energy and drive can still come from the top, eventually you must put in place systems which guarantee that benchmarking will happen automatically. This is done through training programs, selection procedures, performance reviews, and quarterly review meetings. When people stand up in front of their peers and senior executives and give a detailed account of their department's performance, they automatically start to measure their achievements against those of others. After a few of these quarterly reviews, it becomes very clear who is meeting their targets and who isn't. The figures tend to speak for themselves.

It amuses me to think that benchmarking is officially only 20 years old. I worked for a man 30 years ago who set benchmarks for the advertising industry before anyone, aside from surveyors and computer scientists, really knew what the word meant. David Ogilvy was a man far ahead of his time. He invented what he called "Magic Lanterns," which were a set of guidelines for each product to be advertised. They were so successful, they became unofficial industry standards. Many are still in use. Having worked with the Gallup organization, he had a background in research and understood how average people thought. His guidelines were a wonderful tool, because you could share this knowledge with the client.

If we were pitching for an account, we would produce Ogilvy's guidelines about how best to sell that particular product and were soon telling the client things they had never even thought about. For example, Ogilvy discovered that if you were advertising a new toy, the advertisement should never show a little girl playing with the toy by herself. His theory was that boys wouldn't follow girls, but girls would follow boys. The sales figures proved he was right. It was Ogilvy who taught us to sell the sizzle, not the steak. His campaigns are still famous. Remember his advertisement for Rolls-Royce: "What's the loudest thing you can hear in a Rolls-Royce at 60 mph? The ticking of the clock."

If we wanted to break one of his guidelines, we had to have a great reason. If it was a good enough idea or something totally original, Ogilvy would approve it. The campaign, if successful, would be added to the sum of his knowledge and used to set an even higher standard.

Ogilvy believed that winning industry awards came a very poor second to selling a client's product and making money for them. We have won a lot of awards too, but if we aren't making money, what's the point of winning awards? Prizes aren't a particularly good benchmarking tool. Enjoy them, but never kid yourself that because you are winning prizes, your success is guaranteed. Profits aren't everything, but they are a better measure of success than prizes or awards.

Note

[1] Michael J. Spendolini, *The Benchmarking Book* (American Management Association, New York, 1992).

Don't Put Up With Mediocrity

Who gets fired and why and when and even how, goes to the very heart of the character of a company, its management and its leadership. — **Harold Geneen**

If you aren't fired with enthusiasm, you will be fired with enthusiasm. — **Vince Lombardi**

O K, OK, I admit it — I'm a big softy. I *hate* firing people. It's a distressing, unpleasant business — and one that involves coming to terms with your own failings. You have to admit that you made a mistake by hiring the person in the first place. But if you don't fire mediocre performers, you are doomed to failure as an entrepreneur. Just as excellence breeds excellence, mediocrity breeds mediocrity. As Somerset Maugham once observed: "It is a funny thing about life; if you refuse to accept anything but the best, you very often get it."

And so it is with employees. Every business that I'm involved in is pretty cut-throat and only the fittest survive. Passengers taking a free ride at your expense make your business less competitive. If people aren't performing, the sooner you get rid of them the better.

Sometimes people don't keep moving or growing; it's best that such people go, even if they have been with the company a long time. I have never been able to have someone work for me if I don't feel 100% loyalty toward that person. But there have been many times when I have regretted taking so long to remove someone. When I finally acted, I realized that they had been holding us back.

The toughest decision I had to make about letting someone go was in 1997, during the Asian crisis. We had to respond to wave after wave of problems that were threatening to destroy the business. One very senior executive refused to believe that we had to act quickly and wanted to sit tight and wait for the crisis to pass. In my view, this approach was suicide, but there was nothing I could do to persuade him otherwise. So, he had to go. He had been with the company for years and had done good work in the past; what made it worse was I liked him. But this was a matter of survival. I did it in the nicest possible way, with generous severance payments and benefits to soften the blow. We even threw him a farewell party. I believe it is important to give the person as much "face" as possible in these difficult circumstances. Humiliating people in public doesn't achieve much except to give you a bad name.

The crisis created many interesting challenges. Some Thai companies said they would rather go under than fire 20% of their staff. Like the *Titanic*, they all went down together. The thinking behind this stance was that if you fire one in five on the payroll, those sacked are being held responsible for everyone's failings and that isn't fair.

Other companies were proud to say they had never had to lay off a single person. There was a joke going around Bangkok in 1997 that one new and very expensive publishing venture had so many passengers, they should have started a bus company. It soon became painfully clear that some of the senior, highly paid staff couldn't do the job they were hired to do. But rather than face reality, the management simply ignored the problem and hoped it would go away. The boss didn't want to admit he had made a mistake in hiring these people, some of whom were his friends. The group went broke.

Other companies introduced salary cuts for all members of staff in an attempt to reduce costs. Quite often, this was done at the request of staff who would rather take a cut in pay than see their colleagues thrown out of work. During the crisis, we chose a different path. We didn't have any salary cuts, despite requests from our employees. Instead, we took a long look at our staff and decided it was important to get rid of the weak links. We identified the passengers who were taking a free ride on our corporate bus and removed them. That way, we were helping to strengthen the company in the long term rather than merely resorting to short-term measures to survive.

It is equally important when you have outstanding people working for you, to ensure that they stay. Our group has a good reputation for both attracting really bright people and keeping them. It's all about team building: if you keep the stars and fire the non-performers, you build a stronger team because you have removed the weak links. We are one of the largest companies in Thailand — 12,000 employees — not to have a unionized workforce. I believe this is because we have a reputation for fairness.

It shows the importance of training and developing people. One of the biggest changes I have witnessed is the influence of the human resources department. For years, I didn't pay much attention to what was then called the personnel department. Ten years ago, I would have said the most important people on the payroll were in sales. Today, I would say the human resource staff are our key players.

We have a senior executive, a Thai woman, who interviews many of the expatriate executives. She asks them about their goals, explains our bonus schemes, and helps them to develop their strengths and recognize their weaknesses. Her services are invaluable, as she helps to build people. When she started, there was a good deal of resentment toward her; Thai women can still find it tough in the executive world. She is now regarded as one of our most powerful executives — she is our CPO (Chief People Person)! Apart from helping to find the right people, human resources also prevents us from making too many mistakes. We pay ten months' severance pay these days for people who have been with the company for three years or more, so we can't afford to make mistakes with the people we hire.

I have always found it interesting to look at how other people view the problem of firing people. In seeking inspiration, I sought the views of some of the great names in world business. I like the approach taken by Bill Marriott, chairman and chief executive of the Marriott group. In 1990, during the recession, the bottom dropped out of the real estate market in the United States; the following year the Gulf War broke out. Marriott, one of the largest real estate developers in the U.S. who was opening at least one new hotel every week, was hurting badly. The company decided to fire the 1,000 employees who worked in the development and architecture departments.

As a company renowned for its generous treatment of employees, Marriott softened the blow as much as it could. The management brought in a team to help the departing staff find work elsewhere. They helped them to prepare résumés, conducted job searches, and coached them in interview techniques. Marriott wrote in his book, *The Spirit to Serve, Marriott's Way*:

When the lay-offs were announced, we braced ourselves. Not surprisingly, the anger of being laid off often translates into litigation and we had been warned that despite our efforts to provide for our employees, we weren't going to be immune. The concern turned out to be groundless. Out of more than 1,000 people only two took legal action against us, and those claims were minor and amicably resolved. In fact, I was touched when a number of departing employees took the trouble to thank us for our outplacement help. I was likewise pleased that we ultimately were able to place more than 90 percent of those looking for jobs.[1]

Among those who share their thoughts in *The Book of Leadership Wisdom* is Akio Morita, the founder of Sony. He loathes the idea of mass redundancies.

> *One of these outsiders came into an American company, closed down several factories, laid off thousands of employees and was hailed by other executives in articles in the* Wall Street Journal *as a great manager. In Japan such a performance would be considered a disgrace. Closing factories and firing employees and changing corporate direction in a business slump may be the expedient and convenient thing to do and may make the balance sheet look better at the end of the next quarter but it destroys the company spirit. And when the business rebounds, where will the company go to get experienced workers who will produce quality goods and work hard and loyally for the company?*[2]

T. Boone Pickens, one of the most feared corporate raiders in the United States, has this to offer:

> *Of course you make hiring mistakes, and people sometimes have to be fired. I'll live with a bad situation just long enough to know there's no other choice. The rest, believe it or not, is easy. People know when they are not doing the job and the kindest thing to do is to release them.*[3]

But one of the most cogent views on the subject is put forward by Harold Geneen, the tough, no-nonsense former chairman of ITT, who turned the company into a communications giant:

The firing line is perhaps the most acute test. Who gets fired and why and when and even how, goes to the very heart of the character of a company, its management and its leadership. Firing people is always difficult. It's the moment of truth for a business leader. You never face the problem of firing somebody without truthfully, honestly examining the question of how much you yourself have contributed to the situation. Are you firing because the company is under pressure to cut costs, because of general economic conditions, or because you are losing business and market share? If so, then it isn't his fault, it's yours. You were supposed to run the company so that it would be strong enough to weather bad economic conditions and be smart enough not to be caught in the crunch of new products or marketing trends.

You may be firing him because he has done a poor job. But have you asked yourself: "Did he do a bad job because he wasn't helped?" If he could not do the job alone, you were supposed to be smart enough to be able to help him. The most difficult task of all is firing a man who is working hard, doing the best he can but whose confidence in himself far outstrips his abilities. He's over his head. His judgment or lack of judgment might even be a serious danger to the whole operation. It breaks your heart to have to tell such a man that he is incompetent. After all, you probably gave him raises and promotions for ten years.

Or consider the man who has faithfully served the company for 20 or 30 years and now is in failing health and ability. He is only two or three years away from retirement. What would you do with him? There is no simple formula for firing people. There will always be exceptions to every rule. How you handle each of the above cases, however, will determine what kind of leader you are, how much respect you command and deserve from your colleagues, and ultimately the personality and character of the company you lead.

You have to take action. You have to clear the decks for all the other people who are performing up to your standards and perhaps are carrying the extra burden of those who are not. They expect it of you. In physics it is well known that for every action there is a reaction. Every time a chief executive takes an action for or against someone in the company, either firing or promoting a man, there is a reaction throughout the company.

So you have to let all these people go — except for that last fellow so close to retirement. He has earned the right to stay on in his job, even at the expense of efficiency. Perhaps you can move him laterally somewhere, so that someone else can take over his former position. He knows the score. So do all the others around him. If you fired him, the message would be clear: It's the company policy to pay you as long as you are useful and then throw you on the junk heap when you're old and grey. As for the others, it is your duty to let them go, however unpleasant it may be. But you can do it as decently and painlessly as possible.

Ultimately, a good leader should do the decent thing. He should know what the decent thing is. No one wants his or her leader to be tolerant of incompetence through ignorance, indecisiveness or weakness. No one wants to follow a weak leader. He is the worst kind.

You cannot rely upon his judgment because you don't know what he will do in a difficult situation. Much more respect and loyalty is given to a tough leader, the one who is not afraid to make difficult and even unpopular decisions, just as long as he is perceived to be decent and fair and reliable in his dealings with his subordinates.[4]

Geneen died in 1997, but his words are a wonderful legacy for the budding entrepreneur.

Notes

[1] J.W. Marriott, *The Spirit to Serve, Marriott's Way* (HarperBusiness, New York, 1997).

[2] Peter Krass (ed.), *The Book of Leadership Wisdom* (John Wiley & Sons, New York, 1998).

[3] Peter Krass (ed.), *The Book of Business Wisdom* (John Wiley & Sons, New York, 1997), p. 159.

[4] Krass, *The Book of Leadership Wisdom*, op. cit., p. 9.

Rule

18

Chase Quality, Not Dollars

Perhaps it is a gift rather than a quality — a gift of being able to distinguish between that which is ordinary and something that other people will recognize as outstanding, as exceptional.

— Anon

Quality is never an accident; it is always the result of high intention, sincere effort, intelligent direction, and skilful execution. It represents the wise choice of many alternatives.

— Willa Foster

N o successful, self-made entrepreneur has as his or her top priority the accumulation of a fortune. It is the process of making the money — the competition, the challenge of winning at the game of business — not the money itself, that provides the buzz. I have heard people say: "I'm going to do this, this, and this, and I'm going to make $5 million within two years." Such an approach is misguided. If you have a good idea, the first thing you have to prove is that you can make it work. Too many people focus just on the money-making aspect of it, without concentrating on the end product.

Bill Gates has this to say about making money:

Even today, what interests me isn't making money per se.
If I had to choose between my job and having great
wealth, I'd choose the job. It's a much bigger thrill to lead
a team of thousands of talented bright people than it is
to have a big bank account. I'm pretty good at
multiplication, but I never look at the stock price so I
don't know what number to multiply by.[1]

In 1999, Gates's fortune was estimated to be in excess of US$100 billion.

While not in the same ballpark as Mr. Microsoft, I do adopt the same approach. When the stock market was soaring and the economy booming, I woke up a number of times several million dollars richer on paper. On other days, depending on the market, I would be poorer by a million or two. If you are going to build a successful business, it is essential to take a long-term view and not just concentrate on the short-term gains.

In the hotel industry, you *have* to take a long-term view. It can take up to ten years to get a return on an investment in a high-quality project in Thailand. Hotels take time, effort, and energy. At the start, there is the maze of financing and contracts; then construction starts, and you watch nervously as a hole in the ground starts to take shape, foundations become buildings, and the project becomes something you can reach out and touch. That is one of the joys of this grueling but ultimately rewarding process, even if at times it feels like you are running a series of marathons in the hot season.

Yet, despite all the trouble, building a quality hotel is worth it. The Regent Chiang Mai brings me joy every time I visit. At Hua Hin, I love to stroll around the Anantara Resort and Spa, which was built in 1984 as the Royal Garden Village. It's not our grandest hotel, but it's one of my favorites. The design is exquisitely Thai, built low-rise around lush gardens dotted with artworks and furniture from Chiang Mai. We lavished millions on the gardens — the frangipani blossoms give off a beautiful scent — so when you wake up and look around, you are surrounded by the sights, sounds, and smells of Thailand. The hotel employs scores of gardeners who are very proud of what they create. And their pride in their work shows. The hotel, which has won awards for excellence, has done good business since the day it opened. Within eight years, it was highly profitable.

Having set ourselves high standards, we do everything in our power to maintain them. We keep upgrading no matter how difficult things get, because service and facilities can start going downhill very quickly. When times are hard, we take a few deep breaths and say, "Where do we want to be with this hotel when we emerge from the crisis?" We want to be the best hotel in Hua Hin, and we won't achieve that by cutting costs and taking short cuts with quality.

Charles Randall wrote in *The Folklore of Management*:

> *When a sudden fury of ill-considered cost slashing sweeps through a company, "We must cut overheads" becomes the slogan. To many it is a simple command to cut off, overnight, every expense that does not pay off at once. Hack away the intangibles. Forget the future. Have no thought for human values. Give up planning for the long term. Stop construction. Permit no nonsensical talk about the overdue paint job. Cut inventory to the bone, even though it means shutting down the plant of a loyal supplier. We must resist both over expansion in the booms and overzealous cutbacks in the pauses. Let us learn a lesson from the French peasant and his vineyard. He knows that he must keep at his pruning in the spring if the picking basket is to be full in the fall but he never trims off so much that he damages the vines.*[2]

Prune a quality hotel back too far and you can inflict permanent damage. If you want to compete with the best, you have to worry and fret about every detail. The average person coming from Europe is amazed to find that they can live in complete luxury for as little as US$75 a day. Competition is tough, but if the standard of service and attention to detail exceeds expectations, you are halfway to winning customer loyalty. Some of our guests have been coming back to our hotels every year since they opened. If you get the little things right — the massage on the beach, the generously proportioned jacuzzi, or the great service — the rest will fall into place. But maintaining high standards requires great effort. If I notice that dining tables haven't been set properly, or the Irish coffee isn't being made at the table, I fire off a memo and then check to see that something has been done about it. Woe betide the manager who doesn't have a good excuse if something hasn't been improved or put right. I find that my managers adopt the same tactics with their staff, and this has a positive knock-on effect all the way down to the humblest kitchenhand. We are very service-oriented, so we have to get things right. The aim is 100% customer satisfaction: we want *everyone* who stays at one of our hotels to go away happy. Word of mouth can be a far more powerful marketing tool than advertising.

Before he set up the Ford Motor Company, Henry Ford had some dealings with a group of businessmen who were not to his liking. He said of the experience:

> *The most surprising feature of business as it was conducted was the large attention given to finance and the small attention to service. That seemed to me to be reversing the natural process which is that the money should come as the result of work and not before the work. The money influence — the pressure to make a profit on an investment — and its consequent neglect of or skimping of work and hence of service showed itself to me in many ways. It seemed to be at the bottom of most troubles.*[3]

Within the Hua Hin hotel complex we built some beautiful condominiums. They all sold very quickly, whereas many others in the area — mostly highrise monstrosities — lay empty. Why? I think it's because we put a lot of effort into building something we were really proud of. Many condos were built at the time simply to make money. I could have followed suit, but money isn't everything. I think this is where Thailand went wrong: the greed factor crept in. Sometimes it takes an outsider to point out something that is staring everyone in the face — Thai architecture is breathtakingly beautiful. Yet, 15 years ago, few Thai resorts took much interest in gardens or traditional Thai architecture. Cheap bungalows or highrise blocks were the order of the day. Developers looked at concrete condo blocks in Hawaii and then built carbon copies in Thailand.

These highrise condos have hurt the economy and helped to create the property bubble which, in turn, helped to trigger the crash of 1997. They use a tremendous amount of electricity and water, but provide no employment. We employ hundreds of people in our hotels. We buy vast amounts of fresh fish and vegetables from the local markets. We are major taxpayers. Today, we are perhaps the largest taxpayers in the cities of Pattaya and Hua Hin. We represent a significant part of the economy and give something back. This is part of what went wrong in Thailand. People didn't make their investments productive. The purchase of land is only a small percentage of most developments, yet hotels were built along Bangkok's side roads, which provide little or no access, because the land was cheap. Land costs normally account for only 10–15% of the total cost of a hotel project.

In Hua Hin, they chopped down hundreds of beautiful old trees to build a road that was unnecessary. It was a crazy thing to do. Some of those trees were planted in the time of King Rama V, more than a century ago. The avenue of trees helped to give Hua Hin its wonderfully relaxed atmosphere.

There is nothing we have ever done that I am afraid to show people. The greatest mistake you can make is to do something just for the sake of making money. You must build quality projects that will last, and that will make everyone associated with them feel proud. I'm not suggesting that you should be irresponsible in your spending, but quality will outweigh quantity every time.

In a crisis, it is better to control your expenses than to slash costs across the board. You can make a lot of mistakes and still recover if you run an efficient operation. The entrepreneur who controls his expenses better than his rivals will achieve a competitive advantage, especially when he or she demands the highest standards of quality and service at the same time.

Notes

[1] Janet Lowe, *Bill Gates Speaks* (John Wiley & Sons, New York, 1998).
[2] Charles Randall, *The Folklore of Management* (John Wiley & Sons, New York, 1997).
[3] Peter Krass (ed.), *The Book of Business Wisdom* (John Wiley & Sons, New York, 1997), p. 336.

Rule

19

Act Quickly In A Crisis

There is no limit to how bad things can get. — **Murphy's Law**

Adversity reveals genius, prosperity conceals it. — **Horace**

I will remember July 2, 1997, for as long as I live. On that day a series of events was set in motion that threatened to destroy everything I had built in Thailand. Before dawn, senior Thai government officials were summoned to an urgent meeting at the Bank of Thailand. There, the horrible truth was revealed: the country was nearly broke. Attempts to defend the baht had failed; the only option was to let the currency float. The deadly Molotov cocktail of a property bubble, government corruption and incompetence, and lack of transparency in the big financial institutions had finally exploded. It emerged that officials at the Bank of Thailand had already squandered more than US$30 billion in a futile attempt to defend the baht, reducing Thailand's foreign currency reserves to an all-time low. The bank had spent billions more bailing out banks and finance companies. The prime minister, Chavalit Yongchaiyudh, and the governor of the Bank of Thailand, Dr Chaiyawat Wilbulsdi, resigned, but by then the country's economy was in meltdown. The first Asian domino had fallen and within weeks the whole region was in crisis. Malaysia, Indonesia, the Philippines, and South Korea soon went the same way. Even the superstar economies of Hong Kong and Singapore soon lurched into recession. The United States and Europe watched, waited, and trembled as the crisis threatened to inflict great damage on their economies in turn.

In Bangkok, the International Monetary Fund's "medical team" flew in and forced the country to swallow some very unpleasant medicine. The side effects were a painful mix of sky-high interest rates, a liquidity crunch, huge lay-offs, and mountains of non-performing bank loans. For years, the baht had been one of the most stable currencies in Asia, rarely budging far from 25 to the greenback. In January 1998 it hit 56, and many said it was heading for 70 or even 100 to the dollar.

The Stock Exchange of Thailand index had fallen from a peak of 1700 in the mid-1990s to below 250. The general feeling in the market was that at least 50% of the publicly listed companies in Thailand would disappear. Before long, the corporate landscape started to resemble an abattoir. Huge amounts of wealth were destroyed, and some of the great families were ruined. Many business owners simply froze. "We'll wait until the trouble passes," was something you heard a lot. Nobody, including me, anticipated just how bad the crisis would get.

When the news broke, I was on my way back from Hong Kong, where I had been attending the handover celebrations marking the return of the British colony to China, so I had time on the flight to contemplate my strategy. So, what did we do? First, we looked on the bright side. We had already taken some precautionary measures by repaying US$35 million of the group's U.S. dollar debt before the fall of the baht. We had seen the stormclouds gathering. When a government starts declaring that it won't devalue the currency, as the Thai government had declared, and you have got hedge funds betting against the baht, you know what's coming, and it's all bad. Most of us realized that there had to be a devaluation, but we expected the baht to fall only to 30 or 32 to the dollar.

Then I liquidated everything I had outside the country, a nest egg I had accumulated over 30 years, and brought the capital to Thailand to provide support for our companies. I had enough money outside Thailand to retire and live comfortably for the rest of my years elsewhere. But would I be happy doing that? No. So, I had all my eggs in one basket again, just as I had when I started the company. It was all riding on Thailand. I sold my Corvette and my E-type Jaguar, and took a second mortgage on my house.

It was a humbling time for me. Suddenly, as a major

shareholder who had chosen to receive only a nominal salary from my companies, I was receiving no dividends. I was carrying a lot of personal debts and had no way of servicing them. I had no income and huge overheads. I couldn't sell my shares, because many of them were mortgaged to the banks and the value of those shares had plummeted as the stock market had nosedived. Technically, I was broke. I went to our board and said: "Look, I haven't been paid a real salary for ten years. Times have changed. I owe a lot of money. I need to get paid a reasonable salary." I didn't think it was an unreasonable request. After all, I was running the company and working every hour of the day to keep it afloat. They agreed and immediately started paying me a monthly salary. In 1999, the compensation committee increased my salary enormously and also gave me a huge bonus. I got a bigger raise than anyone else and a bigger bonus. Even *my* performance was being measured! I have to admit I was quite pleased that my efforts were being recognized.

My next move was to get our team to pull in the same direction. This was no time for leadership by committee and I had a serious disagreement with one of our senior executives. He took the view that the baht couldn't fall beyond 32 and, if it did, it didn't matter because all of corporate Thailand would be history anyway. He told me: "Your company has been in business for 30 years, so why do you have to react so quickly? Why don't you wait three months?" I told him if we waited three months, the company might not be here. How can you sit around and wait when the currency is falling like a stone? We were holding debt of around US$60–70 million, so every time the exchange rate fell by one baht we lost US$1 million. He left. I had no choice.

We took the following steps.

- We hedged our U.S. dollar debt as much as we could, but there weren't enough U.S. dollars to go around, as many companies were scrambling to do the same thing. We minimized the damage but still took some very big hits.

- We froze all the salaries of all our executives and told them there would be no bonuses. Those people being paid in dollars were told they would be paid in baht at 27.5 to the dollar. We told them, "If you want to quit, we'll understand. But if you want to hang in, we'll give you share options as compensation." We didn't lose a single expatriate executive. My brother Skip was suddenly making less money than he had earned 20 years ago in California.

- I instructed all our managers to take a hard look at their staff. I told them we had to remove the bottom 10%. The non-performers and the passengers had to go. I told them not to fire the last people to join, as so many other people were doing. The last-in, first-out principle doesn't work for me, as it doesn't evaluate performance. Why fire someone who is good just because they were the last to join the company? At one of our restaurants that employed 20 people we sacked the two poorest-performing employees and suffered no loss of service or efficiency. Managers told their staff that we were in trouble and that everyone had to lift their game.

- We overhauled our pricing strategy in the restaurants. Our goal was to bring prices down. We knew that consumers would have less money, so they would have to see great value before they would part with any of it. When the crisis started in 1997, the cheapest pizza you could buy at Pizza Hut was 149 baht, which, at 25 baht to the dollar, was US$6. In July 1998, we dropped the price to 99 baht, which was less than US$3 at the exchange rates of the day. The pizza was the same size; it just had fewer toppings and less cheese. We still made a profit, though less than we had formerly because our margins had shrunk. Our market share increased enormously — 28 million customers, up from 22 million the year before — but sales only rose 7%. Our strategy was the same with Swensen's, where for a month we reduced prices to what they had been when we opened ten years earlier — 12 baht (about 30 cents) a scoop. Baskin Robbins and Haagen Dazs thought we were nuts! However, we still made a profit, attracted swarms of customers, and created great business for our ice cream factory. The result was that we emerged from the crisis with a greater market share in a new market where customers were more confident to spend and absorb price increases.

- We changed our hotel room rates from baht to U.S. dollars. It was a very unpopular move and we were criticized for it in the press, but we had no choice. We needed hard currency. Every single travel agent was selling in dollars, and they wanted to pay us with the sinking baht! Then they delayed paying us because they were waiting for the baht to fall further.

- We closed down several non-core companies that were unprofitable. We also outsourced things like security, maintenance, and cleaning. We became lean and mean and focused on what we did best.

- We sold our 49% stake in Boots Thailand back to Boots, and a 39% stake in Lancôme Thailand to Lancôme Paris, to raise cash.

- We collected our account receivables as quickly as we could. The chain of debt was getting longer every day, so we wanted to get in first. We rushed to liquidate inventories, at any cost. We sold everything we could to raise cash — desks, old computers, cars, trucks — anything that would fetch a dollar. At that time it was almost impossible to borrow, and if you found a lender the interest rates were insane.

Then we hung on and tried to weather the storm. The darkest moment came in January 1998, when the baht went past 55 and there were no bank loans available. Our company lost a lot of its value and I lost a paper fortune. By one estimate I was worth US$100 million in 1996; soon after the crash I was worth perhaps nothing. In 1996, our companies made 300 million baht (US$12 million), our best year ever. In 1997, we lost 1 billion baht (over US$30 million). That meant we needed three of our best-ever years to get ahead again. Throw in rocketing interest rates and a disappearing baht, and the numbers became pretty scary.

I kept telling our staff to keep their chins up. When I started the business with a US$1,200 loan in 1967, I was paying compound interest that was the equivalent of 60% a year. At the height of the crisis we were paying 30%. No company can afford to pay those interest rates for very long, but it was half the rate I had paid initially. I told everyone that if I could survive then, we could survive now.

And survive we did, by following some pretty basic rules:

- Always be positive. Your staff expect you to lead them when the going gets tough.
- Determine what your priorities are, keep your focus on them, and act quickly. Our priorities were to survive, stabilize, and grow.
- Have confidence in your team, and use crises as a learning experience. Everyone should be better at what they do when you come through it.

Little by little, things started to turn around. Tourists were flocking to Thailand. Our share price started to creep up, and the cash flow from our hotels and fast-food operations gave us a little breathing space. In early 1998, we placed shares worth 650 million baht (nearly US$20 million) in a falling market. We were able to raise money during a very difficult time, because people believed we were handling the crisis well. People saw us as survivors, so they were willing to invest in us. We used the increased capital to grow the company. We bought 25% of the Regent Hotel in Bangkok, kept increasing the number of our restaurants, and continued to pay off debt.

There is no question that I was under more pressure and worked harder in those two years than for a long, long time. It was quite an ordeal, but those companies who have survived it, come out stronger, more efficient, and transparent. In fact, 1998 was the best year in the history of our company; as a group, we made almost 500 million baht (around US$15 million). It is a tribute to all our executives and staff.

I feel confident that Thailand will emerge from the recent crisis with a sounder economy. It will prove to have been a turning point for the country, as well as for those companies that survived the ordeal. In our businesses, we are attempting to create a new corporate culture. Senior executives now require junior executives to set their own objectives. Many staff are allowed to award their own bonuses of up to eight weeks based on the objectives and targets they set themselves. The annual one-month bonus is gone; instead, staff can make an extra 8.3% every month if we hit our target numbers. While these practices may be fairly standard in the United States, it is a ground-breaking development for Thailand.

It is essential to keep raising the bar at every level of your operation. For example, in our food operation, we have instructed all our employees to lift their game. If they want to receive a bonus, they will have to meet our performance targets each month. This is the new reality. The iron rice bowl has been broken.

After we had turned the corner, I had the opportunity to read the views of the late J. Paul Getty, oil tycoon and one of the richest men in the world. In an essay called "The Businessman at Bay,"[1] he advised taking the following measures in a crisis:

- No matter what happens, don't panic. The panic-stricken individual cannot think or act effectively.
- Examine every factor in the situation with meticulous care. Weigh up every possible course of action. Marshall all the available resources — cerebral as well as financial, creative as well as practical.
- Plan countermoves with great care and in great detail, yet make allowance for alternative courses in the event of unforeseen obstacles. Ensure that your plans are consistent with the resources you have available and that your goals are attainable.
- Act confidently, purposefully, aggressively and, above all, enthusiastically. There can be no hesitation — and it is here that the determination, personality, and energy of the leader counts the most.

Getty argued that the business person who follows these principles after suffering a reverse will not remain at bay for very long. I think we passed the test with flying colors.

Note

[1]   Peter Krass (ed.), *The Book of Leadership Wisdom* (John Wiley & Sons, New York, 1998), p. 120.

Rule

✦

20

After A Fall, Get back In The Saddle Quickly

Problems are only opportunities in work clothes.

— Henry J. Kaiser

For me, the Asian crisis was over the moment the battle for the Regent Bangkok began in March 1999. After all the pain of the previous two years, suddenly I felt confident enough to take a short break to race a Ferrari in France and to go into the ring with Goldman Sachs and Co., one of the world's biggest investment banks. While conglomerates crumbled and banks went bust in Thailand, our hotel group, fast-food operations, and other ventures had fought their way out of the red and into record profits in 1998. Although analysts predicted economic growth for Thailand in 1999 and applauded the stable Thai baht and recent stock market surges, few companies matched our performance. We enjoyed a 24% growth in revenue for our hotels, and our 246 food outlets attracted five million more customers. From a loss of 1 billion baht in 1997 for our group, our three publicly listed companies made a record 500 million baht in after-tax profit in 1998, with an even stronger first-quarter showing in 1999.

We were in great shape again and I was ready for action. The Regent Bangkok is one of the great hotels of Asia and I had always had a soft spot for the place. Now the companies that controlled it, like so many others in Thailand, had fallen on hard times and needed to sell. The Regent was owned by Rajadamri plc, which in turn was 32% owned by a bankrupt Japanese company, which in turn was being represented by a large Japanese bank.

There was another, more important, factor. The Rajadamri Hotel Company also owned 26% of our six-star hotel in northern Thailand, the Regent Chiang Mai. We didn't want outsiders treading on that hallowed ground. For us, taking another slice of the Regent Bangkok in early 1999 seemed the right thing to do — we already owned nearly 25%.

This was a battle where I had to call on everything I had ever learnt and more: trusting my intuition, using an established network of contacts, using the best brains available to me, and devising new strategies in a rapidly changing situation. If you like, this battle was a microcosm of all the rules I have been talking about. I would be testing my skills against a formidable adversary.

They don't come much bigger than Goldman Sachs, the New York-based investment banking and brokerage giant which participates in major financial markets on behalf of corporations, institutions, governments, and individuals worldwide. Founded in 1869, Goldman Sachs today has 13,000 staff in 41 offices in 23 countries. The bank is a leading investor in the hotel industry, with major stakes in Starwood Hotels, the owner and operator of the Westin and Sheraton groups, among others.

Goldman Sachs had been on the prowl in Asia for some time. In June 1997, it paid US$29 million for 30% of Dusit Thani, Thailand's largest publicly traded hotel company and owner of the famous hotel of the same name just a mile down the road from the Regent. And then, on April 12, 1999, a Goldman Sachs company signed a memorandum of understanding to invest US$500 million to take a 20% stake in South Korea's Kookmin Bank. In 2002, the company sold most of its holding, making a healthy profit in the process.

Henry Cornell, who supervises Goldman Sachs' equity investments in Asia, made it very clear where he stood on the Regent Bangkok right from the start. He told the *New York Times:* "You don't get an opportunity anywhere in the world, really, to buy a five-star existing property because people tend to hold them for dear life. This is a spectacular company with great assets."

It was also a battle of great significance, because the fact that it was taking place at all showed that investors thought there was something in Thailand worth fighting over again. "This is the first takeover battle in Thailand since the crash," Anil Thadani, the chairman of Schroder Capital Partners, a private investment firm in Singapore who owns a stake in the Royal Garden Resort, told the *New York Times* in the same article. "Hopefully, it marks the reawakening of investor interest in Thailand."

The Regent Bangkok has always held a special place in my heart. It was opened in 1983, first as the Peninsula Hotel. It was then taken over in 1985 by Regent, which in turn was taken over by Four Seasons in 1992. In 1983, I was still a novice in the hotel business. I had cut my teeth on converting a rundown collection of bungalows in Pattaya into a going concern and had taken a modest step forward by building our first property in Hua Hin. M.L. Usni Pramoj of His Majesty the King's Private Property Office, is chairman of the Regent as well as chairman of our Hua Hin hotels. We would often dine in one of the Regent's sumptuous restaurants and I could only look around in awe. What a hotel! They had spent over US$200,000 on each room in 1983 when they built it, a huge amount at the time. Our investment in Hua Hin, by contrast, was only $25,000 per room. The gulf between the two was so enormous that every time I visited the Regent I dared not even dream about ever owning even a part of such a property.

But my love affair with the place isn't just based on happy memories. Today, from the moment you walk into the lobby where you can admire the hand-painted silk ceiling as you sip a US$40 glass of Armagnac, you know this is no ordinary hotel. Managed by the elite Four Seasons group, the Regent Bangkok is the perfect base for the five-star business traveler who wants to be pampered. It sits on Rajadamri Road, one of the city's most famous thoroughfares, linking business, entertainment, shopping, and cultural centers. The hotel faces an eighteen-hole golf course and a race course, all part of the prestigious Royal Bangkok Sports Club.

The winner of a host of awards, the hotel boasts 356 rooms and suites which all ooze comfort and sophistication. Each has Internet access, and if you have your own laptop no local service provider is needed. The Regent Club provides a 24-hour business service and private rooms for those who wish to hold negotiations or prepare for important presentations. A lovely touch is the "Cabana" class of room, which offers pampered guests a resort atmosphere in the middle of the city. Guests have their own private patio overlooking a lotus pond and 25-metre swimming pool. There is a ratio of three members of staff for every guest. It is quite simply a masterpiece of the hotelier's art.

More importantly, perhaps, it is also a profitable venture. Immediately after the crash the hotel suffered heavy losses through exposure to U.S. dollar loans. The Regent was hardly alone in that. I, like so many others, had also fallen into that trap. But now the Regent was back in the black and had a rosy future. During the Asian crisis the hotel was packed with business people, lawyers, and bankers who flew in to help Thailand sort out its debt-ridden banks and companies. While Bangkok was awash in red ink and empty hotels, the Regent had thrived. But this wasn't just about money. There were other forces at work. The Regent was a very Thai hotel, and I and other minority shareholders believed it should be kept in Thai hands.

The first shot in the battle with Goldman Sachs had actually been fired back in early 1998. It was then that the first 20% of the shares came on the market. We, in the form of our hotel company, Royal Garden Resort plc, beat Goldman Sachs to the punch and bought the lot for 25 baht a share. Over the next year we increased our stake to 24.8%, below the trigger point of 25% for having to make a general offer for all the shares.

Another 32% of the shares were owned by EIE, a troubled Japanese company, which, through its bank which had control over the shares, announced in February 1999 that it was going to offer the shares for sale in a worldwide tender and politely invited us to make a bid. Suddenly, everyone was knocking on our door, including Goldman Sachs, who wanted us as partners in this bid.

We declined, saying that if we were going to bid we would go it alone. My great concern was that if it went to a simple auction, the shares would simply go to the highest bidder. We didn't have the deepest pockets, especially when compared with people like Goldman Sachs, Morgan Stanley, and other major companies who had indicated they would bid.

We looked at our options. If we wanted control, we would need 51% of the shares. We went to see the other large local shareholders, the Crown Property Bureau, His Majesty the King's Private Property Office, and Thai Farmers' Bank, the second biggest bank in the country. We had done business with all of them before and had found them to be excellent partners. Between them they owned 20% of the Regent shares and we asked them if they would be willing to sell to us. That would have given us 45% — not enough for control, but much closer than before. They declined, but said they would support us at board level and not sell to anyone else. They urged us to try to buy the Japanese shares, or at least sufficient shares, to ensure that control remained in Thai hands.

This meant that if we could get our hands on another 6% of the shares, we would be as good as in control. This close relationship also meant that if Goldman Sachs or any other company bought the 32% held by the Japanese and became the largest single shareholder, we could ensure that, in effect, they had almost no power. We hoped that this would also make the potential auction and the whole issue of owning the Regent a very unattractive proposition. We also let it be known that Thai Farmers' Bank would be prepared to lend us the money to buy more shares. This let all bidders know that one of the key minority shareholders was very much on our side.

We then threw all the bidders another curve ball. We bid for only 10%, instead of trying to go for the auction. The thinking behind this was that we wanted to make the Japanese shares less attractive so that they could never be used to get a controlling shareholding. If our bid resulted in just 6% of the shareholders either selling to us or not selling to anyone else, we would, with our Thai friends, have effective control of the hotel.

We talked up the plan with our friends in the media, saying that with our existing shares, those of the friendly minority shareholders, and this extra 10%, we would be home and dry. We also made it clear that if the Japanese sold to anyone else, we would regard this as hostile. It worked. We launched our bid at 25 baht, up from the market price of 20.

The Japanese arrived in town and we sat down to a very tough round of negotiations. They admitted the auction had been disappointing due to our strategy. They said they had been offered as much as 35 baht a share on the condition that representation on the board was guaranteed and subject to due diligence. We said we would resist that. We told them that as a publicly listed company, prospective buyers could get the information from market analysts. Remember, we were trying to make it as difficult as possible for them to sell to anyone else. The strategy seemed to have merit and we came to an agreement on March 16. We had a deal at 27 baht a share to buy from the Japanese. I went home a happy man, thinking the deal was done. That was a big mistake.

On March 25, the Japanese turned round and reported they would not sell to us. On the same day, Goldman Sachs announced a tender offer for a minimum of 26% and a maximum of 100% at 38 baht. We then knew that Goldman were going to try to take the shares promised to us by the Japanese. We fought to ensure the Japanese delivered on their commitment. Finally, on April 5, Goldman announced it had bought the 32% shares from the Japanese for 38 baht. The deal was worth US$14 million and cleared the way for a general offer to all shareholders at 38 baht by Goldman.

I was stunned. I heard the news on my return from Singapore, before attending a classical concert at the Regent Hotel. I have to admit my mind wasn't on the music that night. Immediately after the concert, I called a strategy meeting with Anil Thadani, my key advisor, and we talked long into the night. What were we going to do?

Ten years ago, I wouldn't have even dreamed of going 15 rounds with one of the world's great investment heavyweights. Back then, I simply didn't have the knowhow or the nerve. The easiest option was to sell out to Goldman and make a large amount of money for our company. What the hell, deals are like buses: another one will always come along soon. But I loved the Regent. I had enjoyed many a fine bottle of wine there with family and friends. I didn't want to sell, especially to people I considered to be "outsiders." At the same time, I was keenly aware that I mustn't allow my love of a particular hotel to interfere with good business practice. A bidding war with the world's largest investment bank wasn't a good idea.

Ego can be a dangerous thing, especially when there is a lot of emotion tied up with a deal. Goldman would always beat us if it was simply a matter of cash. I had to make the distinction between good business sense and wanting to own one of the great hotels of the world.

It was time to introduce Plan B. The next day, we announced we would up our bid to 42 baht for the 10% of the shares we needed in order to get control of the Regent with the other friendly minority shareholders. It was a defensive strategy designed to keep us in the ball game. At this point Goldman Sachs had 32%, Royal Garden Resort 25%, Thai Farmers' Bank 8%, Crown Property Bureau 7%, and our good friends the King's Private Property Office 6%. The remaining 22% of shares were closely held by families who might be reluctant to sell at any price. I just hoped they wouldn't sell to the "wrong" team. Our advantage was we only had to bid for 10%, while Goldman had to keep bidding for 100%.

Goldman reacted a week later with an increased offer of 43 baht for 15% of the shares. If more than 15% of the shares were tendered, each shareholder would receive a weighted average price of between 38 and 43 baht. This was a clever strategy. By attaching the condition that it wouldn't buy more than 15% at the top price of 43 baht, Goldman Sachs protected itself from having to pay top dollar for an avalanche of shares if we decided to sell, but it wasn't so good for us.

In May, as this drama was unfolding, the first-quarter results for the Royal Garden Resort, our publicly listed hotel company, were released. They made interesting reading. Pre-tax profits rose 44% over the same period in 1998 to 93.3 million baht. Occupancy rates were nudging 90%, and room rates were up between 20% and 30%. Hotels — at least *our* hotels — were good news again in Thailand.

With the other minority shareholders, we agreed to allow Goldman to take over the three board seats the Japanese shareholders had held previously, but the chairman stated they must not make further attempts to gain majority control. That offer fell on deaf ears and Goldman continued its hostile takeover for majority control.

On June 3, both sides made their last move for the Regent Bangkok. We responded with a slightly increased bid of 43 baht per share (matching Goldman) for 10%, at the request of the other Thai shareholders, in order not to engage in a bidding war with Goldman. Goldman, however, wasn't going to give up and went all out with a new final bid of 48 baht. Under Thai stock market rules, both offers were final and shareholders had until June 24 to decide what to do. It was a long three weeks and the result was what I expected — a stalemate — but one that we believed was to our advantage. Goldman Sachs managed to buy just over 8%, taking its stake to 40.5%. We increased our position to 27.5% — an amazing feat, considering our price was 5 baht less, but perhaps it was an indication of the support our bid enjoyed. I put out a press statement immediately. "We're very happy to see that Goldman has been unsuccessful in their hostile takeover bid. We're very happy with the fact that we were able to keep the Regent Hotel independent of any single shareholder." Goldman put out a statement too. "We will work closely with all other directors and the management team to ensure that the company has a clear and focused growth strategy that builds long-term shareholder value," said a Goldman spokesman, I would like to think through gritted teeth.

Goldman Sachs, one of the most powerful financial organizations on the planet, may be the biggest individual shareholder of the Regent Bangkok, but that doesn't mean it can call the shots. This is what Anil Thadani told an interviewer after the dust had settled:

> *The two tender offers were very well covered in the media — which portrayed RGR and Bill, as the local underdog, if you will, and Goldman as the big American predator – using their financial muscle to try and take control of a Thai institution. The episode really underscored several of Bill's qualities and key strengths. The groundswell of support for Bill and RGR in Thailand was very touching. In the end, of course, Goldman's bid to acquire control was not successful. The episode really underscored a sense of national pride that seems to exist in Thailand, more than other Southeast Asian countries — and Bill's ability to use his track record, charisma and personality to rally shareholders to his cause.*

Despite the battle for control, we have developed a good working relationship with the Goldman executives. The Regent has undergone major renovations and is now even more profitable. A million dollars was spent on the lobby alone and we have added two superb western restaurants — if you want to eat the best steak in town or enjoy five-star Italian food, just head for the Regent.

Goldman got involved just to make money. We got involved because we love the hotel, its staff and its history. I believe that one day we will buy Goldman Sachs out and then the destiny of this beautiful hotel will be completely in our own hands.

That wouldn't be a bad result for a kid who has never been to college.

Rule

21

Fight The Good Fight (Especially Those That You Can Win): Pizza Wars – Act I

Things turn out best for the people who make the best of the way things turn out.

> — ***Anon***

A pessimist sees the difficulty in every opportunity; an optimist sees the opportunity in every difficulty.

> — ***Winston Churchill***

Earlier in the book, I spoke about the need to embrace change because it is the one constant in the business world. However, sometimes we don't move fast enough or look hard enough to recognize change until it has embraced us first. Our recent dispute with Pizza Hut is proof of this.

In 1998 and 1999, our Pizza Hut sales experienced little growth. Although we controlled over 90% of the pizza market in Thailand through our 116 outlets, a lack of competition and the lingering effects of the economic recession capped growth in what was our largest food service operation. Our other operations such as Dairy Queen and Swensen's were expanding rapidly, but we needed another big food service success story if the company was to keep moving forward.

Chicken was the obvious choice. We estimated that, on average, Thais consume only 60 grams of pizza per person per year, but they eat nearly 12 kilograms of chicken. In Malaysia consumption rises to over 26 kg and reaches 54 kg in Hong Kong. Chicken has always been the primary source of protein in the Southeast Asian diet and is readily available.

As early as 1995, we approached Pepsi-Co, the then owner of KFC who also owned Pizza Hut, for the opportunity to operate KFC restaurants in either Thailand or somewhere else in Asia. It became clear that the company wished to operate this brand itself and so we began to look elsewhere for a concept that would appeal to both the Thai and to the broader Asian market.

In 1997, we began trials of Australian ready-to-eat chicken dishes called Chicken Treat. Based in Perth, Chicken Treat was founded and is still owned by long-time food service operators. It is the leader in the Western Australia market and is now expanding into South Australia. Our trials and consumer testing in 1997 were very promising, but the economic recession that began in July 1997 put all of our expansion plans on hold.

In early 1999, with an economic recovery underway, we reopened discussions with Chicken Treat. In October, 1999, we signed an agreement to develop the Thai, Malaysian and Singaporean markets. The hard work to introduce Chicken Treat was just beginning.

At around the same time, we also found ourselves facing negotiations for a new Pizza Hut franchise agreement. Our existing agreement was signed in 1990 and we understood it involved an initial term of 10 years with the right to renew this agreement for five more years subject to a change in the royalty. The franchise agreement with Pizza Hut only restricted us from operating another pizza concept in our territory, so the chicken deal should not have been a problem.

We knew that throughout the world many Pizza Hut operators had other restaurant concepts, including chicken and hamburgers, and faced no difficulties with Pizza Hut on this issue. KFC also appeared little concerned about other restaurant concepts. In Thailand alone, KFC had been involved since the early 1990s in a joint venture with CP Group to own and operate KFC restaurants in Thailand. CP Group also owned and operated two of its own ready-to-eat chicken concepts, named Chester's Grill and Five Star Chicken.

In the U.S., franchisers are required to file copies of their agreements with government agencies. When we reviewed the standard agreements then being offered to new Pizza Hut franchisees in America, we saw that they were being asked to agree not to compete in the pizza segment and were also given a minimum exclusive area of one mile around their restaurant in which the franchiser would locate no other Pizza Hut. This trade zone protection is a key protection for a franchisee to ensure that they have sufficient time to recoup their investment without the threat that another same-brand restaurant locates nearby to cannibalize their customers. The agreement being offered by Pizza Hut to its American franchisees mirrored our existing agreement and was what we believed would be offered to us.

We were wrong. Things had changed.

In late 1997, Pepsi-Co spun off Pizza Hut, KFC and Taco Bell into a company called Tricon Global Restaurants. Tricon has a simple plan – to dominate the world's fast-food business. The company "succeeded". By 2002 it had changed its name to Yum! and was operating more than 30,000 fast-food outlets in over 100 countries around the world. Systemwide revenues for 2001 were US$22 billion! We were dealing with the proverbial 400 lb gorilla that was used to sitting exactly where it liked.

And so it proved. In its non-American operations, Tricon began to change the previous business relationship between franchisee and franchiser by requiring the franchisee to commit to what it considered a loyalty to all the brands that it owned, instead of just the one that the franchisee had a commercial relationship with.

In mid-1998, we began discussions for a new long-term franchise agreement to cover the period beyond January 2000, should we not exercise our five-year renewal rights. The franchise agreement presented to us was very different from both our existing agreement and the agreement then being offered to new Pizza Hut franchisees in the U.S. In summary, Tricon was asking for an eventual 50% increase in the royalty to 6% of sales from 4%, a 100% increase in the "initial fee" for new and renewing stores, $17,500 to $35,000 per store and eliminating all trade zone protection in our franchise agreement. In addition, we would be barred from entering the chicken, hamburger, Mexican and pizza segments at either the retail or wholesale level not only in Thailand, but also anywhere in the world. Furthermore, we would have to seek Tricon's permission before we could enter any other food business anywhere in the world. Acceptance of these outrageous terms would have reduced our ability to grow as a public company, and could have made us a quasi subsidiary of Tricon without it investing in us.

To put this in perspective, a New York Pizza Hut operator operating under a U.S. Pizza Hut franchise agreement could come to Thailand and open a Domino's, a Popeye's, and a Taco Time and never be in violation of his agreement. However, as a Pizza Hut operator in Thailand, we could not open a Burger King or chicken restaurant in Thailand or anywhere in the world. Furthermore, we could not even open a Thai restaurant in New York or Thailand without Tricon's permission!

Given the dramatic changes from both the previous agreement and what was then being offered to Pizza Hut franchisees in the U.S., we were unable to reach an agreement with Tricon in 1998 and 1999. We even considered forming a joint venture to combine our Pizza Hut outlets with Tricon's KFC outlets, but Tricon wanted 51% and management of any joint venture. This was unacceptable to us because we would have been unable to consolidate the largest part of our publicly listed company's revenues and its large cash flow, and we would have been dependent only on dividends. This last prospect was the most worrying, as Tricon's track record in Thailand was not very impressive.

KFC is the largest single restaurant brand in Thailand with more than 250 outlets, with 150 owned by Tricon. However, in spite of being the dominant market player, the Tricon KFC operation in Thailand had not recorded any significant profits. According to publicly available documents, in 1999, Tricon's KFC operation had sales of 1,930 million baht (US$42.9 million), assets of 1,600 million baht (US$35.6 million), but lost 46 million baht (US$1 million). During the same year, our Pizza Hut sales were around 1,800 million baht (US$40 million), but we had only 1,300 million baht (US$29 million) in assets and harvested a profit of around 90 million baht (US$2 million). We were achieving the same level of sales using two-thirds of the assets, and taking out a substantial profit even after paying franchise fees that were not charged to Tricon's own stores. We believed that we should manage the joint venture because we had demonstrated an ability to deliver profits to shareholders, whereas the managers of Tricon's KFC operations had not. However, Tricon remained steadfast that it should manage any joint venture in its own way.

We said to Tricon: look, let's agree on everything else and come back to the problem clause later. We agreed to invest US$50 million and open another 120 Pizza Hut restaurants over five years. This was a big commitment for us to make. We also agreed to the increase in royalty payments from 4% of revenues to 6%. In dollar terms, this meant paying Tricon US$3 million a year instead of the US$2 million we paid in 1999. That is big increase, and showed our level of commitment to the deal.

To be honest, I did not worry about this disagreement to begin with. We were still negotiating in good faith and were optimistic that the deal would be signed. I thought it was just part of the negotiating strategy. No American company should be able to dictate terms such as these to a Thai partner. I genuinely believed that common sense would eventually prevail. Unfortunately, it didn't, and things were about to go from bad to worse.

In October, 1999, we decided to exercise our right to renew the agreement for a further five years and also announced our agreement to open Chicken Treat restaurants. We believed that the non-competition clause presented to us wouldn't be allowed in Thailand and asked Tricon to submit it to the Thai government agencies for a ruling on its legality, but it was against seeking this ruling.

Although we continued to maintain a dialogue with Pizza Hut in an attempt to resolve our differences, nothing prepared us for what came next. On November 17, 1999, Tricon took out full page, paid advertisements in three of Thailand's leading newspapers, revealing the state of our negotiations and stating that if we did not come to an agreement on new terms by January 17, 2000, then Tricon would operate Pizza Hut in Thailand itself.

I was outraged. I immediately tried calling a senior Tricon executive in the U.S. but he would not take my calls. I know this guy really well personally and he would not even speak to me! That hurt. I thought to myself: "I have spent 20 years of my life building your Pizza Hut brand and paying you millions of dollars in royalties, and you won't even pick up the phone. What a way to treat people."

I left a message saying I was willing to fly to Tricon's corporate headquarters in Louisville in Kentucky to talk face to face. No one returned my call. The message from Tricon was clear — sign the contract or we won't have anything to do with you. They had declared war on me, my company and my staff.

Our people were in shock. The brand which they loyally built to be the market leader for the past 20 years had stabbed them in the back! Our staff were in tears. They were wondering if they were going to lose their jobs. Our bankers, landlords and suppliers suddenly began questioning the future of the company and its employees who a day earlier had been one of their best customers. Our share price fell by 25% on that same day and over 50% in the next 30 days, as shareholders and analysts questioned a life without Pizza Hut. Over US$50 million in shareholder value evaporated during those 30 days because of that unprecedented and uncalled-for public advertisement. Then the banks started calling to cut our credit lines. Overnight we went from being one of their best customers to credit pariahs.

There was only one thing to do — fight back with our own brand of pizza.

People Build Brands, Brands Do Not Build People: Pizza Wars – Act II

A successful person is one who can lay a firm foundation with the bricks that others throw at him or her.

— David Brinkley

The best executive is the one who has sense enough to pick good men to do what he wants done, and self-restraint enough to keep from meddling with them while they do it.

— Theodore Roosevelt

Never correct a competitor when he is making a mistake.

— Paul Kenny

Y ou have to be either brave or foolish to take on a U.S. corporate giant like Tricon. Perhaps we were a little of both. A protracted legal battle is the option of last resort, especially in the U.S. where legal fees are astronomically high and the process long and demanding. But we felt there was no other option, and so the next 11 months were consumed with fighting for our rights in the New York court that had jurisdiction for the existing franchise agreement.

The battle lines were drawn. We had filed a US$50 million claim for damages. Tricon was seeking to enforce a clause in our agreement that would have required us to stop selling pizza from our existing outlets for a period of 18 months. We believed that Tricon did not offer us the five-year renewal we were entitled to, and so we believed we were released from that obligation and would go our own way.

We were concerned about what would happen when the contract expired on January 21, 2000, as after that date we had no legal right to the name "Pizza Hut". We informed Tricon that we would take down all the Pizza Hut signage and return the pizza recipes and manuals. We would then launch our own brand of pizza in our restaurants.

Tricon immediately got an injunction to stop us taking down the Pizza Hut signs. It was dangerous to ignore a U.S. judge's instruction, although question marks remained over the court's jurisdiction in Thailand. If we refused to comply we would have never received a cent in damages and I would probably have never been able to visit the U.S. again without being served with a lawsuit. We honored the judge's ruling and left the Pizza Hut signs where they were. We remained open for business.

Then things started to get a little weird. Tricon started building its own Pizza Huts, sometimes right next to ours. We went to the judge in New York and put a stop to new Pizza Huts being built alongside ones that we were already operating.

One of the many things I learnt during this time was that lawsuits in the U.S. are a real roller coaster ride. One moment it looks like you are going to win and be awarded US$50 million in damages. (At times like these I started dreaming of buying that corporate jet I'd been hankering for.) Then the next day Tricon would get a ruling, and suddenly everything would look bad again.

As the day of the trial drew near, I was spending more and more time with a jury consultant. Every time I was taken through the drama of what happened, my emotions got the better of me and I burst into tears. It was completely spontaneous. The reality of what was at stake was finally dawning on me. You spend 20 years building up a business that has thousands of employees and 95% of the market. Then the company that owns the brand that you have made so successful takes it away from you, and at the same time destroys your share price and a substantial chunk of your personal fortune. They were grim days and I was becoming a physical wreck. I wasn't sleeping properly, my weight dropped 15 kilograms and I developed stomach ulcers.

But I still felt that we were right and we would win. Almost from day one, the judge had granted us the right to a jury trial. We felt that the man in the street, the jury, would be on our side when they heard what Tricon had done to us. We were confident the jurors would see how badly we had been bullied by this corporate giant and award us substantial damages.

Then the day before the trial was due to start, the judge called our legal team in and dropped another bombshell. We were not to show the newspaper advertisements that Tricon placed in the newspapers to the jury. Our lawyers were horrified. They told the judge that it was these advertisements that had started the whole thing. It was like not showing the gun that the killer had used to shoot the victim. The Tricon lawyers knew just how damaging those ads were and had somehow convinced the judge they would prejudice the jury.

Just as we were coming to terms with this decision, the judge announced that there was no need for a jury. She would hear the case and make a ruling. We were devastated. We had been banking on pleading our case in front of a jury all along. Now our fate was to be decided by a single judge. Who knew what could happen? The judge could rule that we could have another five-year franchise with Pizza Hut. That would be a disaster, because after five years we would be faced once again with oblivion. In the meantime, Tricon would be building Pizza Huts all over Thailand while still collecting royalties from us.

It was just too risky. In November 2000 we settled out of court, over US$2 million poorer in legal fees. In summary, we would continue to operate our 116 outlets as Pizza Huts until January 2001. We would then close our restaurants for 45 days to rebrand them as "The Pizza Company", and train our staff with our own recipes and products. Tricon would then be the sole operator of Pizza Hut in Thailand and we would compete against each other in the market. But this still gave Tricon a massive advantage. For 45 days it would be the only show in town, time enough to press home the huge advantage I had supplied by capturing 95% of the market for Pizza Hut for the last 20 years.

Now the real battle began. We were now faced not only with the loss of a brand that we had pioneered in Thailand and nurtured for more than 20 years, but also with the Herculean task of creating almost overnight a viable competitor to ensure that we would survive as a company.

The media, competitors and even friends in the food service sector around the world told Paul Kenny, the CEO of our publicly listed food company, and I that the launch of a new brand on this scale against a competitor with 95% market share and an unlimited budget had never been done before and simply was not possible. However, they didn't know that our 4,000 pizza restaurant staff had no alternative but to prove them and the world wrong. This was our secret weapon.

They were extraordinary times. Every trace of Pizza Hut disappeared from all our 116 restaurants in a single day. The signs came down all over the country. They were replaced with big stickers in the windows that said simply: "COMING SOON — THE PIZZA COMPANY".

All our people stayed. No-one quit, despite Tricon offering increased salaries to lure them over to Pizza Hut. All the part-time delivery drivers simply waited for us to reopen. The staff loyalty was simply amazing. They knew exactly what the odds were, but still chose to stay and fight. The feelings against Tricon ran high. Tricon was telling the media that the success of Pizza Hut was down to its brand, not to our people. This was a huge slap in the face, and served to rally our staff.

The 45 days between closing down as Pizza Hut and reopening as The Pizza Company were sheer pandemonium. It was an enormous challenge. We had to create our own range of pizzas, rebrand more than 116 restaurants all over the country, design new menus, and at the same time keep waging a publicity war in the media and generally try to stay sane. There were many 18-hour days as the deadline for the re-launch approached.

We worked relentlessly not just to create a good pizza concept for the local market, but to create the world's best pizza concept. With a clean canvas in front of us, we had no restrictions, and ideas poured in from our staff and our customers.

For years our customers had told us that they wanted more variety, and thicker sauce and toppings. We heard them, and developed 30 varieties of pizza with thick, juicy toppings and a rich tomato sauce. Although experts said it couldn't be done, Paul Kenny and his team of loyal experts created one dough blend for three types of crust, while competitors use three dough blends. We created new appetizers such as *bruschetti* to complement the Italian theme of our restaurants and enhance the dine-in atmosphere.

The end product was the result of the collective knowledge, experience and, most importantly, passion of our people. Passion can never be taught, given or bought. You either have it or you don't. Our people have heaps of it, and it is evident in every facet of our business.

In the middle of all this mayhem we received a huge boost to our morale when the banks gave us a new credit line of US$20 million, which we desperately needed. How did we do it? Simple. We invited them to come and try our pizza and compare it to that of Pizza Hut! Several senior bankers told me afterwards that they were willing to bet on us because they were so impressed by the complete commitment of the staff they talked to. They thought our pizza was pretty good, too.

After six weeks of renovation and training, our 116 outlets were to open officially for business on March 17, 2001. Although we then knew we had the best pizza, the best staff and the best locations, we also knew that we were going to open with a brand and products unknown to the Thai consumer. Would people come to try our pizza?

The Pizza War was about to begin. Here is what *Time* magazine had to say about the impending battle:

Hannibal had his elephants, Rommel had his Panzers and Bill Heinecke has his pizzas. And the pizza war is every bit as brutal as those fought by bow or musket or machine gun ... Analysts around Asia are watching to see if Heinecke, the man who built Pizza Hut into the stomach-share king of the nascent Thai pizza market, can mount a challenge to his former employer. More than a few analysts think Heinecke could be leading his bakers and bikers into a sausage and anchovie Agincourt.[1]

Thanks for nothing. It wasn't exactly what I wanted to read at that moment.

The battle with Tricon was sucking every last bit of energy out of me. There were times when I was intensely depressed. I had everything tied up in the company; the share price had collapsed, so any wealth that I had was in danger of being completely wiped out. I started asking myself: How do you start again at 53? At 30 you can start again, perhaps at 40 too. Even with a great résumé and a great story to tell, would it be possible to get someone to back you and start from scratch? The answer was that I didn't want to find out. That thought drove me even harder to succeed.

The night before the launch, we held a private party. One of Thailand's most respected politicians, Dr Supachai Panitchpakdi, who on September 1, 2002, became Director-General of the World Trade Organization, made an impassioned speech in praise of free trade. He said that times had changed — for example, everyone knew that the best Peking Duck no longer came from Beijing. It was to be found here in Thailand. Why shouldn't The Pizza Company go on to make the best pizza in the world?

That night was one of the longest of my life and I don't

think I slept a wink. The next morning, Saturday, March 17, we held a rally at 6 a.m. for all the part-time delivery staff who — we hoped — were going to come back to work for us. I rode to the rally on my Harley Davidson and all I could think about was: "What if nobody shows up?" My fears were unfounded. There was a sea of 700 motorcyclists waiting, all raring to go in their new red "The Pizza Company" uniforms. It brought tears to my eyes.

We were ready, but was the public? The radio and television advertising slots started at 11 a.m. as the doors of The Pizza Company restaurants were thrown open around the country. We held our breath and waited. Within minutes we knew we were onto a winner. The public response was extraordinary. People poured into the restaurants to try our pizzas.

From the time we first opened our new nationwide telephone number, "1112", that morning, to the time we closed at midnight, the telephones never stopped ringing and the seats at the dine-in restaurants were full. The delivery service could not keep up with demand. Our advertising, our image and our food had struck an immediate bond with consumers.

We had another ace up our sleeve: we owned our huge customer database. If you had ordered a pizza we knew where you lived. It sounds like an insignificant detail, but it proved to be enormously important. During the 45 days when Pizza Hut was the only show in town, thousands of orders had been messed up. This was particularly true in Bangkok, a city where addresses are notoriously difficult to locate and, of course, the biggest market in the country. As soon as we opened for business, we knew exactly where all our customers were. We had our own telephone call center staffed by people who really cared about The Pizza Company. Pizza Hut outsourced its delivery and call center to third-party vendors who could never be as committed as our staff.

In the first two weeks after we opened, our sales were over 60% higher on a same-store basis than they were a year earlier, even though the economy was slower and our major competitor now had 70 outlets and was outspending us three-to-one on advertising dollars. Our staff set new records for both revenues and numbers of pizzas served. We couldn't keep up with the demand, and even had to pull out our advertising after only three days because it was like putting gasoline on a fire. The overwhelming demand made it nearly impossible to meet our guaranteed 30-minute delivery, but most customers, when told of the delays, still asked for the orders to be filled even if it meant waiting longer than usual. We quickly recruited extra delivery drivers to keep up with surging demand. For deliveries that failed to make it on time, we later offered complimentary pizzas.

Even after the excitement and promotions of our launch period had ended, the positive same store-sales continued. We continued to add new appetizers such as *calamari*, as well as new pizzas like *tom yum goong* (the famous Thai spicy soup) and *tempura* pizza to further enhance the public's positive association of The Pizza Company with innovation, quality, variety and value. For the first time in two years, we also started thinking again about new store development. Although it was early, we had clearly proved that The Pizza Company was here to stay and would be a worthy competitor to the world's largest restaurant operator in the world.

Tricon had been waiting for us to collapse, and yet the opposite had happened. Look at the numbers. The Pizza Company went from zero market share to 75% in the first month, way above our target figure of 50%. Pizza Hut had slumped from 95% (when we ran it) to 25% — despite having a 45-day window when the brand had the market to itself.

Here are the economics of Pizza Hut today:

- It collected a check from us every quarter for 20 years. In our last year, we paid the company over US$2 million.
- It never had to spend a dollar on advertising until it declared war on us.
- It is now losing an estimated US$10 million a year on its new operation in Thailand.
- Tricon has invested US$50 million, yet is losing US$10 million a year. We believe it wants to sell its Pizza Hut operations to a new franchisee.

I am sure there are a few red faces around at Yum! During the legal battle we offered to sell them the company for US$100 million. It would have broken my heart to do so but I had to face up to the possibility that selling might be the best way out of the mess. We estimated our profits of over $5 million annually plus over US$2 million of royalties. Tricon declined the offer. If it had accepted our offer at least Tricon would have been a profitable going concern in Thailand.

To give you an example of how flawed Tricon management thinking was, consider this. In 2000, Anil Thadani managed to sell the KFC chain he owned in Taiwan back to Tricon for what Anil described as "a very good price in excess of US$60 million". The 60-restaurant chain was losing US$5 million a year.

It is interesting to note that Tricon's entire board of directors at the time owned less than 1% of the company. They make millions of dollars in benefits but own almost no shares. I own half of my company. That's why I'm willing to put my money where my mouth is. I kept threatening to come over to Tricon shareholder meetings and ask how, in Thailand, the company went from having 95% of the pizza market to 25% overnight; or why it used to receive US$2 million in royalties but now is losing money. (Tricon doesn't like to talk about this much. I wonder why.)

I look back and try to analyze why were we successful. We were new and different. When we opened for business everyone wanted to try our pizza. In the first two weeks our sales were 65% higher than the same period the previous year when we were running Pizza Hut. Our "buy one pizza get one free" initial promotion was an amazing success. We also had a sympathy vote. Tricon had received a lot of bad publicity. We were the small Thai company being threatened by this huge American corporation. We also had our customer database, which proved crucial. I believe there are still some Tricon Pizza Hut drivers out there trying to find the right address to which to deliver their pizza orders!

In 2001 the Minor Food Group publicly listed company lost 224 million baht (about US$5.5 million), mainly because of legal fees and the rebranding costs. We understand that Tricon operations in Thailand lost US$10 million. In the first quarter of 2002, Minor Food Group made almost US$500,000 on record turnover — the first profit for six quarters. We have turned the corner. Tricon is now trying to sell its operations to get out of the very same mess that it created. Most of the people involved in the "pizza wars" have now left Tricon.

The dispute over the Pizza Hut franchise agreement and the resulting birth of The Pizza Company taught me many lessons. During more than 20 years of building the Pizza Hut brand in Thailand, it had never occurred to me that our people and I would ever *not* be associated with it. However, during the dispute and in the period prior to opening The Pizza Company, it became crystal clear to me that what made the brand was our people.

Brands are only as good as their people and their passion for excellence. In a few short weeks, our people had created a brand, an image and a menu that had taken on and surpassed the world's largest pizza brand. Despite having an open checkbook, Pizza Hut's market share fell from 95% to 25% literally overnight. Although I still believed in the power of branding, especially global brands, I had just witnessed confirmation that even dominant brands also must be constantly reinvented through the infusion of fresh new blood and ideas. Our people had great ideas about their pizza restaurant business, but were limited in the past as to what they could do. Now they amply demonstrated what they were capable of when given the freedom to do it.

I started to look around at all of our various businesses in this new light to see if we were letting our people work to their full potential. As I looked around, I was able to sleep much better knowing that the people I worked with were masters of their craft, and that the brand in their hands was only one of the many tools that they possessed. While a powerful tool, a brand is only as good as the people using it — and if you have chosen the right people, they can just as easily create a new brand and even, in some cases, fashion a better one if asked.

In a nutshell, people build brands, brands don't build people. The Pizza Company is testimony to this and its success can never be taken away from the people who built it.

---

[1] *Time* magazine, April 9, 2001, International edition.

Rule

$\leftarrow\!\!\blacklozenge\!\!\rightarrow$

23

Be Prepared For Anything:
The September 11 Rule

We can't control every event but we can control our response to it.
— Ken Blanchard

Who will ever forget where they were on September 11, 2001? I had come home late from the office and was slumped in front of the TV watching a movie. Our maid rushed in and said a bomb had exploded in the World Trade Center. I switched over to CNN just in time to see the second plane smash into the second tower. Soon afterwards, the famous landmark disintegrated before my eyes. It was one of the few occasions in my life that I found it hard to believe what I was seeing. The sheer enormity of the horror was difficult to absorb. My emotions seesawed between outrage, disbelief and fear; between utter loathing for the people responsible and a helpless pity for the victims.

September 11 changed everything. It altered the normal patterns of human life for everyone — those of us in the tourist industry included. I had another crisis on my hands. People did not just stop flying. They stopped traveling. In fact, they stopped doing just about anything. Seminars and conferences were cancelled. Official dinners were postponed indefinitely. Everything simply ground to a halt.

For someone in the tourist business, the consequences were devastating. Our hotels emptied almost overnight. We were hit by wave after wave of cancellations. The American and Japanese tourists simply stayed home.

At least one American was determined to carry on as if nothing had happened — my mother Connie. I called her that night to tell her what was going on. She lives in Hua Hin, a resort about a couple of hours drive from Bangkok, and was scheduled to fly to Europe the next day to meet up with her sister in Athens. They were booked on a cruise of the Aegean. I suggested she might want to cancel the trip — I mean, who knew what was going to happen next? She waved away my protests even after her sister had called from the U.S. to say she was not able to come over to Europe because all flights were grounded. "How dare she stand me up?" yelled my mother, who was 82 at the time. "I'm not going to let some terrorists ruin my trip." And off she went. The hotel was as deserted as the cruise ship but she had a great time.

I became determined not to let terrorists or their actions interfere with my job. Unlike my mother, most of our overseas hotel guests were reluctant to travel and our hotels were not busy places! The high-end business at the Regent Chiang Mai and the Regent Bangkok was suffering horribly and the resorts were not doing much better. Occupancy rates were sliding to potentially ruinous levels. Travel agents immediately told us that we had to bring our prices down. I ignored them. This crisis had nothing to do with cost. It was all about security. I was proved right when the European tourists started returning in some numbers in October. I think Europeans are more used to terrorism as many have lived with it in some form for much of their lives.

But on September 12 we were standing on the edge of a cliff. We simply had no idea when the tourists would start returning, or when — and if — businessmen would start flying again.

There was another complication. We were just getting back on our feet after the bruising battle with Tricon over the Pizza Hut franchise (described in chapters 21 and 22). Although we had emerged as winners, the "pizza wars" had sapped a lot of our financial strength. The share price of Minor Food Group (MFG), the publicly listed company that ran our pizza business, had taken a real hit because investors were unsure if we could survive the bullyboy tactics being used by the American corporation. Well we did, and we believed the low share price presented a great opportunity for us to strengthen and shape our own destiny. In July, our publicly listed hotel affiliate, Royal Garden Resort plc (RGR), made a tender offer for 30% of MFG shares.

We had been considering this strategy ever since the share price dropped to below 30 baht following the dispute with Tricon. The two companies seemed a good match, as MFG owns the Pizza Company chain and other fast-food brands such as Burger King, Swensen's, Sizzler, and Dairy Queen, and food and beverage sales accounted for 40% of RGR's total revenue the previous year. Furthermore, MFG operates restaurants and outlets in virtually all airports in Thailand, giving it a direct play on the tourism sector. We put out a statement saying that the purchase of 30% of MFG would complement the long-term plans of both companies to expand their operations, both in Thailand and abroad. After all, we were about to open our eighth hotel, the 265-room JW Marriott Resort and Spa in Phuket. There were also longer-term plans to build a new resort on Koh Samui, a beautiful island in the Gulf of Thailand.

Let me put it this way, it seemed like a good idea at the time.

The first offer price of 40 baht was cautious and conservative, to test the waters. MFG was selling for 42 baht at the time and we wanted to see what the response was like from the market. Initially, nobody wanted to sell, which we took as vote of confidence. Investors did not want to part with their shares because they believed the value would increase as we returned to profitability after the Tricon affair. Indeed, some market analysts were quoted in the press as saying that they believed MFG's shares would go as high as 70 baht inside 12 months. In late August, MFG's share price had risen to 45.75 baht, and we increased the tender offer to 52 baht, which attracted strong interest from sellers. To us, it looked like a good deal that would value the company at less than US$50 million, the price of building our new hotel in Phuket. The tender period was to close on September 20 and everything was looking good.

Then September 11 happened. Suddenly, everyone wanted out — 99% of shareholders wanted to sell their shares at 52 baht. As soon as the market reopened the MFG share price plunged to below 30 baht. We tried to pull out but despite our appeals that circumstances had changed beyond all recognition — a fair point, you might think — the Stock Exchange of Thailand made us go through with the tender for 30% of the shares. We had to pay 52 baht for shares that were suddenly worth less than 30 baht. That cost us an extra US$6 million.

To say that this was a bad time to take a hit like that would be a considerable understatement. We were in serious trouble again. We had just been through the wringer with our pizza business. Now the hotel operation was under threat. It all came down to simple arithmetic. Our hotels were emptying, we had lost US$5 million in reservations, revenues were plunging and the share price was going through the floor. Only one thing remained constant — our costs. Even MFG felt the pain as its airport food operations dropped dramatically as flights were cancelled and people stopped traveling following September 11.

I had been here before. In July 1997, the Asian financial crisis swept through Thailand before going on to devastate the rest of the region. The lessons we learned from the 1997 experience proved to be very useful. Many companies did not survive that crisis because they froze and did not act. Those that made it knew they had to switch into crisis management mode immediately. As in 1997, we acted very quickly. The staff had seen what had happened in New York and Washington and knew the scale of the problem, unlike the Asia crisis, which was harder to explain. Staff meetings were called and the message was simple: costs had to come down.

We looked at every penny being spent; from the simple act of turning off an electric light, to a detailed cost analysis of day-to-day operations. The first casualties were all the part-time staff, who were let go immediately. Then we evaluated all the full-time staff. We cleared the ranks of anyone who was not pulling their weight. Some very senior executives lost their jobs. A series of very tough decisions were made but we only wanted to keep the best. It was déjà vu. We were doing everything that we had done in the 1997 crisis all over again. And it worked. We survived.

As best-selling author Ken Blanchard pointed out:

> *We can't control every event but we can control our response to it. Life is unpredictable. What makes a winner is that when something happens that person's belief system brings forth attitudes that can take good events and make them better; likewise, it transforms bad events into opportunities to learn.*[1]

We did learn. The Asian financial crisis was like a long, dark tunnel. You were not sure where and when, or indeed if, you were going to come out the other end. It was complex, messy and globally divisive. After September 11, the whole world pulled together immediately. The war on terrorism was launched and the Taliban and Al Qaeda were kicked out of Afghanistan. After the initial horror, you soon had the feeling that the world was returning to something approaching normality. The crisis passed relatively quickly and we had minimized the amount of damage done to our business.

The other day I was looking back through the most recent Royal Garden Resort plc annual report. Remarkably, 2001 was a good year for our hotel business, with most posting higher earnings than the previous year. Let me share with you some of the results which we achieved in spite of September 11.

- Net profits rose 61%.
- Room yields rose in every hotel.
- The JW Marriott Resort and Spa opened in Phuket.
- Tourist arrivals in Thailand rose 4.8%, to over 10 million.

As I told shareholders at the annual general meeting: "It gives me great pleasure to report another record performance by our company. Our portfolio of leading hotel properties in Thailand recorded a banner year." Not bad for a year when perhaps the worst terrorist attack in modern history paralyzed the world and tourism.

All this underlines Thailand's strengths as a nation. A Buddhist country, there is no terrorism or civil unrest. Many tourists choose not to go to Indonesia or the Philippines any more. Thailand has grown in stature as a place to visit while many of its neighbors have declined. I believe Thailand is now the most important tourist destination in Asia and perhaps one of the most significant in the world. We want to be the market leaders in Thailand, so it is an extremely exciting time.

As a business, we are now leaner and stronger. If we were not, we probably would not be here after going through three major crises in five years — the Asian financial crisis, the "pizza wars" with Tricon, and September 11. I have aged dramatically during this time. The pressure has been enormous. I could have been ruined personally and 12,000 employees who have built the business could have been thrown out of work. The responsibility has been great, but the buck stops with me. It does get a bit lonely sometimes. But you have to win — so many people are depending on you. That is why you have to be prepared for anything.

***

Note

[1] Ken Blanchard and Don Shula, *The Little Book of Coaching* (Harper Collins Business, New York, 2002).

Rule

24

Reinvent Yourself:
Onwards And Upwards

It is not enough to stare up the steps — we must step up the stairs.
— Vince Havner

Seek to renew yourself even when you are hitting home runs.
— Howard Schultz

H oward Schultz, the CEO of Starbucks, personifies the passion, values, and inspiration that drive the successful entrepreneur. His favorite expressions include: "Don't be threatened by people smarter than you," "Compromise anything but your core values," and "Seek to renew yourself even when you are hitting home runs." They all strike a chord with me, but it is the last quote that really hits home. Schultz, who turned coffee into a high-street culture in the United States and then set about conquering the rest of the world, is never satisfied. He is always looking to grow his business to the next level.

Well, so are we. Our strategic thinking has undergone a seismic shift. Everything is changing — our vision, goals, benchmarks, products, properties, and perspectives. Our hotel business is rebranding and forming alliances with Marriott and Four Seasons, two of the industry's superpowers; we have launched Anantara, our own brand of luxury hotel; we have created whole new areas of business by entering and dominating the spa and time-share markets. Our hotel group's credit rating is the best in the hotel and property industry in Thailand, and is higher than that of many of the banks that are lending us money. Our food division has become a franchiser of The Pizza Company and is breaking out of the geographical constraints of Thailand to enter markets as diverse as China, Russia, and the Middle East. We have also made a bold new move in the aviation industry. All our businesses are evolving to meet the challenges of a competitive world market. If you want to continue to grow and be a market leader you have to constantly re-evaluate. Is this the best we can do? How can we make it better? These are the questions you must be asking all the time. A lot of executives perform well for five years but many can't cope with moving to the next level. Staff must grow or they must go.

Consumers are getting smarter and more demanding. It is becoming more difficult to sell a hotel room and if you want to charge another US$20 you had better have something special to offer, or that guest will check in down the road.

Best-selling author Ken Blanchard put it this way:

Today's leading organizations share a commitment to constant improvement. They believe they're going to be better tomorrow than they were yesterday, better next week than last week, better next month than last month and better next year than last year.[1]

Our companies are reaching out, stepping up, expanding and improving in many different directions. We are becoming bigger, better, and more sophisticated. Armed with new ideas, new brands, new standards, and new markets, we are on the move.

Reinventing yourself is an ongoing process, not an event. Some changes are forced on you and others are made by choice. Look at the "pizza wars" We had no intention of creating our own brand until we had to. Now The Pizza Company is established as the market leader in Thailand and is an emerging world brand.

With the hotel group it was a case of sitting down and looking at the big picture. We were a small player on a big stage. We knew that if Royal Garden Resorts, our publicly listed company, wanted to be a major hotel player in 30 years it was time for a radical rethink about the way forward. We have been in the hotel business for more than 20 years. In that time the industry has changed so much it is barely recognizable from the day we started with a few bungalows in Pattaya in 1978. The world is so much more competitive now.

The big names in the hotel business are everywhere in Thailand. It really is a question of embrace change or be left way behind. The intensifying competition triggered by globalization has made branding even more important as rival players jostle to distinguish themselves in an ever more crowded marketplace.

Our target is to become the leading hotel operator in the Asia-Pacific region, not just in Thailand. This requires a quantum leap — so why not go the whole way and change everything — the name, the style, the concept, the brand? In 2001, we took a huge decision to drop our own local brand, Royal Garden Resorts, in favor of Marriott. Our Royal Garden Resorts in Bangkok, Hua Hin and Pattaya are now Marriott Resorts and Spas. This branding strategy will allow us to expand, as the Marriott brand is widely recognized in Europe and the U.S. It also gives us access to Marriott's global reservation system. The strength of the Marriott name is very important, as it is now the leading hotel brand in Thailand today.

The decision caused quite a stir. This is how the re-branding story was reported in the *Bangkok Post*:

> *Royal Garden Resorts seems to have been around since the year dot. In reality the company has less than two decades under its belt, but it has been a smart player in the public relations stakes, creating strong brand awareness with local companies and travelers. But all will change when the Thai-owned firm takes on the Marriott branding at all but one of its properties. Essentially it is a franchise agreement that leaves hotel operations and policy firmly in the owners' hands, while taking advantage of Marriott's global awareness and marketing links. It's a*

> *sign of the times. Local hotel firms recognize they need*
> *stronger global marketing to keep their share of the*
> *tourism cake. What franchising has given Royal Garden*
> *is access to a reservations system and global marketing*
> *support that will give the group's hotels a clear advantage*
> *over other local chains.*[2]

We have always had a good relationship with Marriott. Our partnership shows that I have not gone off the franchise business despite the terrible experience with YUM Brands (formerly Tricon) over Pizza Hut. Business relationships are governed by the people involved — you can have good franchise partners, just as you can have rotten ones. Our relationship with Marriott is excellent and I like the people and the brand. It is a relationship built on mutual respect and trust.

We are also rebranding at the very top end of our business. The Regent Bangkok and the Regent Chiang Mai have become Four Seasons hotels (which also owns the Regent brand name). The new hotel being built on the beautiful Thai island of Koh Samui will also be a Four Seasons and will be pitched right at the top of the market. Bill Bensley, one of the world's best-known hotel designers, will design and landscape the project, as he did for the Regent Chiang Mai.

Aligning ourselves with the great names of the industry — Marriott and Four Seasons — involved taking a giant step. To upgrade our properties to meet their standards required a huge commitment on our part — a commitment in capital and a commitment in quality. We feel confident we have made the right decision.

But we have not stopped there. We have also created Anantara, our own new luxury hotel brand, at the former

Royal Garden Village in Hua Hin, one of my favorite hotels. Anantara is the Sanskrit term for "borderless water" and we aimed to create a very special Thai ambience. Nestled by the beach on the sunrise side of the Gulf of Thailand, Anantara offers a blend of traditional Thai architectural heritage, exotic interiors and natural tropical gardens that has made this resort and spa one of the most romantic hideaways in Southeast Asia. Bathrooms open into bedrooms that open on to expansive terraces overlooking lotus-covered lagoons. Our new hotel made a huge impression on the media and the reviews were sensational. Creating Anantara allows us to put into practice everything we have ever learnt about the hotel industry. We plan to build many more.

The new strategic thinking is already paying dividends. On July 30 2002 Royal Garden Resorts received a credit rating of A — reflecting, the credit agency said, "the dedication and extensive experience of its managements team, the geographic diversity of its properties in major tourism destinations and its good asset quality." We now have the highest credit rating in the hotel and property industry in Thailand. In fact, we have a higher rating than many of the banks lending us money! Our rating is almost as good as the national credit rating of Thailand itself. It is all part of the process of boosting growth and keeping the momentum going.

We are making acquisitions too. In 2002 Royal Garden Resorts bought a luxury hotel in Chiang Rai, the exotic town in the heart of the Golden Triangle, the "badlands" straddling Thailand, Burma and Laos. In the past the area was awash with warlords and drug runners. Today, it is a peaceful and remote retreat from the worries of the world and a perfect place for a luxury hotel. The Baan Boran Chiang Rai is a five-star 110-room property and the acquisition is one of the very few transactions that has taken place in the Thai hotel industry recently. It was a very good opportunity to add to our portfolio, especially as it was already profitable. This too may be rebranded as a Four Seasons property or Anantara. We will be making more acquisitions. In the old days, I steered clear of this strategy because it introduces different corporate cultures into your own company. Now, if we want to continue to grow we have to consider acquisitions, otherwise everything takes too long. You might say, I'm running out of time!

A key part of the success story has been the introduction of spas. We recognized spas as an emerging global trend and jumped in with both feet. Spas are now becoming an integral part of the quality hotel market. The Lanna Spa at the Regent Chiang Mai was voted the number 2 spa in the world by *Travel and Leisure* magazine in 2001, so we are now setting the standards in what has already become a multi-million dollar industry around the world.

I have to chuckle when think I about this. This is a classic example of a simple idea that had been staring me in the face for years. The art of Thai massage is centuries old, practiced through the ages by experts who have handed down their skills to the next generation. Thai massage has extraordinary health benefits that the West is slowly waking up to. Something that used to be considered rather seedy and sleazy has become an integral part of our five-star family resorts. People are flying in from all over the world to experience it. Take me, for example. I'm constantly stressed and have the the aches and pains to be expected of a 53-year-old who has spent too much time racing cars and motorcycles. A massage can make the difference between feeling bad all day or being comfortable and relaxed. It affects my performance as a decision-maker and as a leader.

I remember giving a lecture to a group of 500 university students taking a course in entrepreneurial studies at Mahidol University. At the end of my talk I asked if anyone had any good ideas about what would be the "next big idea". There was silence. Eventually a hand went up right at the back of the hall. "What's your idea?" I asked. "Thai massage," came the reply, accompanied by a chorus of smutty giggles. "That's a very clever idea, and in fact we are looking at Thai massage as we speak," I told the shocked audience, who did not know whether to laugh or applaud.

Our joint venture with Mandara Spa is much, much more than just Thai massage though. The spas feature an array of traditional and herbal treatments delivered in attractive and comfortable environments. Our interiors are furnished with traditional Thai décor and use wood throughout to create a warm and relaxing atmosphere. Soothing sounds, intoxicating aromas — the flavor is distinctly Thai and lusciously tropical. Treatments include various types of massage, body treatments and aromatherapy. Deluxe spa suites are spacious enough for couple to have treatments together. Each includes a large private plunge pool, a steam and shower room, and ensuite bathrooms, and many open into a private tropical garden with outdoor shower and traditional Thai *sala*. Why not feel self-righteously healthy by ordering a typical spa cuisine meal of spinach salad with poached quail's egg, steamed fish on olive couscous or other low-fat, high-fiber dishes? It's the definition of pampered perfection. Today we are the largest spa operator in Thailand with over 15 spas after just three years.

The other radical decision we made was to move into the time-share residential-business. Please don't groan. I know the very mention of the expression "time-share" often conjures up images of fly-by-night salesmen conning people into buying a share of something that has not been built yet and probably never will be. We are the modern, quality face of time-share investment.

This is a completely new industry in Thailand. Again, we are setting the standards. The devastation of the 1997 property crash erased all trace of time-share as a business. Our joint venture Phuket Marriott property is the first time-share property in Asia. Marriott are just plain thrilled with what we have done there. We want to be the best in the world rather than just the best in Thailand.

If you do not believe me, check out Marriott's Phuket Beach Club, which is next to the JW Marriott Resort and Spa. The 144-unit property is part of our five-star resort on a massive estate on Mai Kao Beach in the northwestern part of Phuket. For approximately US$18,000 buyers get to own, for seven days a year, one 119-square-metre, two-bedroom, two-bathroom apartment. The purchase is good for 80 years and owners can pass the rights of this time-share property on to their children. The JW Marriott name means buyers can expect good service and protection against risks that smaller, independent developers often cannot provide. Also, owners of the Phuket Beach Club have immediate access to the numerous worldwide hotels and services that Marriott has to offer. Alternatively, the annual week's holiday you buy in Phuket can be taken at any of the 52 resorts Marriott operates in 29 other destinations worldwide. Why does it work? People recognize a good investment when they see one. The Phuket Beach Club offers a holiday home in one of the prime beach resorts of the world for a modest price. We expect to sell over US$200 million worth of time-share in this project in the next three to four years.

As you can see, we have been very busy on the hotel

front. One of the central themes in the drive to improve and expand is to seek a broader "footprint" for our brands and products. Our business is becoming more international on all fronts. Yet, at the same time, the "Thai-ness" of our products is an increasingly powerful force. This apparent contradiction can be seen in the restaurant business. Thai people are very proud of their cuisine, and they want to see this reflected in our menus. It shows how much Thai society has matured in the last 25 years. Until recently, there was a great desire to experience all things western, especially among the young people. Now there is a great pride in Thai culture and it is those companies that adapt to this process that will succeed. You have to embrace these changes wholeheartedly, not just pay them lip service. We have hired specialists to make sure our Thai food is authentic. We have added a great new "Thai flavor pizza" to The Pizza Company .

Having been a franchisee for so many years it is nice to be on the other side of the fence. We sold our first Pizza Company franchise to a former banker and he is already doing great business. He paid 1.5 million baht (about US$35,000) and will pay us 5% of revenues (remember, I paid US$5,000 for the entire Pizza Hut franchise for Thailand in 1980). This small start is the way forward for us. We plan to have 10 pizza franchisees by the end of 2002. The next step is to go international and our target markets are as far afield as China, Kuwait, Bangladesh, and Russia. We are considering launching our own brand of coffee houses. These days, when we look at a product or an idea, we ask: Can we use this in more than one market, not just in Thailand? This is a big departure from our previous thinking that was focused purely on Thailand.

We are daring to dream of having 1,000 restaurants in five years. Franchising will drive this growth. We will franchise

Swensen's ice cream parlors in Thailand, Vietnam and other parts of Southeast Asia. We are looking at similar plans for Dairy Queen.

In my lifetime I believe that revenue from our franchise business will be greater than that from the restaurants we run. The industry has changed and we have changed with it. Today, the big profits are in the franchise business. When I started with Pizza Hut the margins for the franchisee were generous. Today, competition with the likes of McDonald's and KFC is ferocious and margins have shrunk considerably. If we had kept the relationship with Pizza Hut we would be struggling today because we would be being squeezed from two sides. The franchiser wants a bigger slice of revenues in fees, and the consumer wants a good deal or he will take his business elsewhere.

Our target is to have 100 franchisees in Thailand by 2005. This will help us to continue to dominate the pizza business and will also boost our revenues enormously. We now also have the Burger King franchise which is already turning a profit. Funnily enough, we took over the franchise from rivals Central, who lost money on Burger King. Central now has some of the Pizza Hut franchise that we used to run so successfully, and is finding that being a franchisee of Pizza Hut is not as profitable as it used to be when we had it. It is another sign that we must be doing something right.

Another example of our efforts to "step up" is in aviation. Minor is now the authorized sales representative in Thailand for Cessna aircraft, ending a long relationship with Piper. I love Piper aircraft and still fly one. I've sold quite a few in Thailand over the years. But I always wanted a jet. Cessna makes jets, and that is next! I believe strongly in the concept of private planes playing an important role in business travel.

They can save executives a lot of time and hassle. It was only natural that we had outgrown the Piper agency especially as I wanted to generate more revenue from the aircraft industry. Cessna is a much bigger operation. Piper makes around 250 aircraft a year and generates sales of US$300 million; Cessna makes up to 1,000 with sales of US$2.6 billion. We took over the Cessna franchise in 2001 and are working on the idea of using Bangkok as the center for a charter jet for executives and upmarket travelers. For example, a visitor could get from the beautiful temple complex of Angkor Wat in Cambodia to the Regent Chiang Mai in an hour, spend the night and then fly to the JW Marriott Resort and Spa in Phuket. Try doing that on a commercial airline and see how long it takes! A chartered jet could also be used for emergency medical evacuations, an area sadly overlooked.

All the private jets disappeared from Thailand after the Asia crisis. Wealthy Thais had bought the planes in baht at 25 to the US dollar. They doubled their money by selling them in US dollars at an exchange rate of around 50 baht to the dollar. It's time for people to start buying again.

We are handling all three Cessna ranges: the single-engine piston range, the Caravan multi-purpose turbine range, and the Citation series of business jets. There are seven Citation models suited to various tastes and budgets, starting at around US$4.5 million. A top-of-the-line Citation X can be yours for around $18 million.

But never mind planes, pizzas and products. Only *people* can take us to the next level.

The secret is to have staff who want to keep raising the bar. People are drawn to our company because of our success. We spend a lot more time interviewing people than we used to. It is part of the process of reaching for the next level. We are very tough on new employees, especially in the first six months. The idea is to throw everything at them and see how they perform. If they can handle the pressure you know you have a great employee. Human resources is now a vitally important department in our organization. A lot of people are nervous about joining us because they know how high the pressure is. They are moving from a comfortable environment to one that is intensely challenging.

Our best executives receive three to four big offers from other companies each year. I tell them that if they are not getting offers they have something to think about because they are not being noticed. People have to really want to continue to benchmark themselves against the best. Most of the executives who left us after the September 11 crisis were good, talented people. The problem is that they had become complacent. They had lost their edge, the fire in their belly. You have to get the balance right between great expatriates and the cream of local talent. We are finding more and more Thai talent pushing through. There is a new focus on performance by Thais that was not always there in the past. It is a very good omen.

We are a much stronger group than we were in 1997 before the Asian financial crisis. We are a franchiser as well as a franchisee, we have brands that are now well established, and we have launched new brands. We have diversified but are still focused. We have a new stream of revenues and we have more balance. We used to have too many eggs in one basket — around 70% of all revenues came from Pizza Hut. Today, The Pizza Company accounts for around 35–40% of all revenues. We have done this by driving growth in the other brands while still doing a great job with pizza.

I believe that not only are we in the hottest industries, we are also in one of the strongest regions. Now we are looking much further afield and the focus is on moving outside Thailand. We will soon have a much stronger international flavor than we have had in the last 20 years. We have a much broader network of contacts today. As we have grown bigger and look for greater opportunities Thailand appears to be getting very small. While our first steps into some of these other markets may have been premature — China and Vietnam, for example — we feel the timing is now right. We learned a lot from the earlier experiences. China is the flavor of the month, be it fast food or hotels. China's a major player and has one of the most powerful economies in the world. I also have a better understanding of how the place works after my experiences with Pizza Hut in Beijing in 1989. We already have a hotel in Vietnam and are now distributing Swensen's there. The economy is strengthening and Vietnam is full of opportunities.

I think you are going to see a very dynamic Asian economy over the next few years and our companies are well positioned to take advantage of that. I don't know what it is going to be like as we try to become a world player in some very competitive industries, but we are going down that road to find out!

Note

[1] Ken Blanchard and Don Shula, *The Little Book of Coaching* (Harper Collins Business, New York, 2002).

[2] *Bangkok Post*, January 18, 2001.

Rule

25

Be Content

In the best of times, our days are numbered anyway. It would be a crime against nature for any generation to take the world crisis so solemnly that it put off enjoying those things for which we were presumably designed in the first place — the opportunity to do good work, to fall in love, to enjoy friends, to hit a ball, to bounce a baby.
— Alistair Cook

Be content with your lot — one cannot be first in everything.
— Aesop

Reflect that life, like every other blessing, derives its value from its use alone.
— Samuel Johnson

When I started out, everyone expected me to fail, to run out of money, to run back home. People told me I was too young to run a business, too young to get married, too young to race cars, too young to be president of the American Chamber of Commerce. Well, I have a successful marriage and two great sons; I've won a lot of events, from rallies to circuit races; I've run a successful business since the age of 18; I became the youngest president of the American Chamber — and I've never had to go back home cap in hand. That was the challenge in 1967 — to prove them all wrong.

On June 4, 2002, I turned 53, and on reflection I have to say that I am satisfied with my lot in life. True happiness doesn't come from getting everything you want, but from being content with what you have. It is about putting everything in perspective. Business success needs to be accompanied by other qualities to be really meaningful. Managing a growing business requires unyielding dedication that can consume the soul, impair the senses, and warp the mind. This can be harmful to the individual, his or her family, and the enterprise. Your ability to deal honestly and fairly with everyone at all times will be your greatest strength, and your ability to lead a full, well-rounded life your most important accomplishment. Success by itself means very little.

A friend of mine, Rik Neville, sent me these thoughts that have been doing the rounds on the Internet. It is unclear who the author is but I'd like to share them with you as the message is a powerful one.

The paradox of our time in history is that we have taller buildings, but shorter tempers wider freeways, but narrower viewpoints. We spend more, but have less; we buy more, but enjoy it less. We have bigger houses and smaller families; more conveniences, but less time; we have more degrees, but less sense; more knowledge, but less judgment; more experts, but more problems; more medicine, but less wellness. We drink too much, smoke too much, spend too recklessly, laugh too little, drive too fast, get too angry too quickly, stay up too late, get up too tired, read too seldom, watch TV too much, and pray too seldom. We have multiplied our possessions, but reduced our values. We talk too much, love too seldom, and hate too often. We've learned how to make a living, but not a life; we've added years to life, not life to years. We've been all the way to the moon and back, but have trouble crossing the street to meet the new neighbor. We've conquered outer space, but not inner space. We've done larger things, but not better things. We've cleaned up the air, but polluted the soul. We've split the atom, but not our prejudice. We write more, but learn less. We plan more, but accomplish less. We've learned to rush, but not to wait. We build more computers to hold more information to produce more copies than ever, but we have less communication. These are the times of fast foods and slow digestion; tall men, and short character; steep profits, and shallow relationships. These are the times of more leisure, but less fun; more kinds of food, but less nutrition. These are days of two incomes, but more divorce, of fancier houses, but broken homes. These are days of quick trips, disposable diapers, throw-away morality, one-night stands, overweight bodies, and pills that do everything from cheer to quiet, to kill. It is a time when there is much in the show window and nothing in the stockroom; a time when technology can bring this letter to you, and a time when you can choose either to share this insight, or to just hit delete.

Work and business may be your passion, but they must never become an obsession or your life will soon be hopelessly unbalanced. You can only do so much. I'm never going to be the richest man in the world. When I was young, I wanted to be the youngest self-made billionaire in the world. But as I grew older, that goal changed. In another five years, I would like to take my foot off the day-to-day pedal. That means finding someone with the same drive, who will work 12 hours a day. I still want to participate, but there are so many other things I still want to accomplish. I want to learn how to fly a jet. I want to set a speed record from Florida to Bangkok in a jet. I can no longer become the first man to circumnavigate the globe in a hot-air balloon, but I can hunt for sunken treasure off the coast of Burma. I have enjoyed becoming a grandfather. Now I want to celebrate every aspect of my life.

I said before the last three crises that in another five years, I would like to step back a bit. That is now a moving target. I have lost a couple of years of progress and growth because of everything that has happened. I'm probably looking at another five-year horizon. I hope I can keep up the pace. It is getting harder. I'm healthy but the body is not quite in the fighting trim that it used to be. The last five years have been exhausting but, I can now say, in principle, satisfying. I thought the fight with Goldman Sachs over the Regent Bangkok was tough until I got into the ring with Tricon over Pizza Hut — a small franchisee getting into the ring with the world's number 1 fast-food company. I underestimated them, but at the same time I think they underestimated me. The experience certainly made me appreciate better everything I have achieved.

In 1996, Forbes estimated that I was worth US$100 million. I'm not sure that I was, but I certainly had a hell of a lot going for me. The economy was booming, our shares were rising — everything in the garden was rosy. Having had a negative nett worth in 1998, it is great to know that we are back in positive territory.

The writer James Michener once observed that: "One who has mastered the art of living simply pursues his vision of excellence at whatever he does, leaving others to decide whether he is working or playing." I do want to spend more time relaxing in ways that will keep my competitive spirit burning. In August 2002 I went out and bought a vintage Ferrari — a 1976 fiberglass 308 GTB. It's a class model and only 712 were made. I sold all my sports and racing cars during the Asian crisis in 1997, but now I want to get back behind the wheel again. I have also ordered a Porsche GT3 that I will drive on the Porsche Classic circuit in Asia. I must be spending a little more time away from the office, as even my golf game is improving!

If anything happened to me tomorrow, I would be satisfied with what I have achieved. I am trying to build something that will survive and be remembered. After I am gone, I want people to ask who created these remarkable hotels with their beautiful gardens. I get great satisfaction from the knowledge that the gardens in our hotels are talked about all over the world. I've had people ask me: "Bill, you've been in the hotel business for over 20 years and you only have nine hotels. What have you been doing?" But I designed and built each of those hotels with loving care. J.W. Marriott runs nearly 2,000 hotels worldwide. I don't envy him because I *don't want* to run 2,000 hotels. I like to lavish love and attention on my hotels. No matter what happens in the future, nothing can take away the fact that I helped create the Regent Chiang Mai. I was the one who got this beautiful hotel built, put the deal together, made it happen. I don't want to be the biggest, but I do want us to be the best at what we do.

I still want to win, but it's not critical to my life anymore. I have set certain boundaries. Most of our business is in Thailand. This is my home. I could have bought Swensen's USA at one time — our royalty payments were big enough to finance the purchase of the company in the U.S. — but I didn't want to have to fly to the other side of the world three times a month. Who needs it? Certainly not me. We are expanding well beyond Thailand but our headquarters will always be here in Bangkok.

My health is excellent, and I want to keep it that way. I believe that if you can sleep well at night, you are in good shape, both physically and mentally. Those people who try to survive on three hours' sleep a night puzzle me. I have yet to meet anyone who can maintain peak performance without sufficient rest. The human body just isn't designed that way.

Looking back, I realize that everything is relative. The pressure I felt losing US$10,000 as a young 18-year-old businessman was as great as I feel today when I lose US$10 million. My tolerance levels for pain and pressure have increased. I'm able to handle much more, because I've been through it all before. It's like the first time I lost money playing poker. It prepared me for the moment when our accountant ran off with US$50,000 and we had to ask the banks not to foreclose on us. And then, of course, came the Asian crisis, which threatened to wipe us out. This crisis, along with the fight with Pizza Hut and the fallout from the September 11 terrorist attacks, have taught me how to handle most challenges that an entrepreneur can expect to face in business.

One day in Chiang Mai, right at the darkest point of the Asian crisis, my wife Kathy asked me why I was so depressed.

I told her I had lost so much money that I was worth less than when I started the company. In one year, I stood to lose everything I had worked for and built over 35 years, Kathy said: "Think about it. Thirty-five years ago we didn't spend our weekends in one of the finest hotels in the world. Things can't be all that bad." Of course, she was right.

It is these sorts of experiences that strengthen one's resolve and nerve. Over the years, adversity has taught me to assess a problem by always looking at the worst-case scenario. What is the worst possible outcome, and can I live with it? When I am cruising in my plane at 25,000 feet on autopilot, I say to myself, "What's the worst that could happen that I have no control over?" The plane could explode, but there would be nothing I could do, so there is little point in worrying about it. But what if we lost cabin pressure? I would have less than a minute to get my emergency oxygen mask on, or I could drop to 14,000 feet where I could breathe the air. I know I could handle that. It's a good strategy in business, too: if you don't think you can stay in control of the situation if something really bad happens, then bail out of the deal.

I have some religious faith. I have prayed for help when times have been hard. My religious upbringing was as a Christian Scientist, which is very much centered around the power of positive thinking. My father was diagnosed with terminal lung cancer when he was 30. The cancer disappeared, and he lived to be 76. He believed that positive thinking had cured him and he became a Christian Scientist. Don't shut faith out of your life. I have experienced many dark moments when thoughts of suicide weren't far away. I needed all my faith in order to hang on.

I have always had faith in Thailand, too. Despite all the coups and crises, I have always believed the country will go on to bigger and better things. It is a very resilient place, and so are its people. We have been through a lot together. In 1975, when Saigon fell to the North Vietnamese, the American military were forced to withdraw from Thailand and everyone thought it was the beginning of the end. Thailand would be the next "domino" to fall to communism. Many people left Thailand fearing the worst, but instead of a Vietnamese invasion, the country was invaded by investors from Japan and elsewhere. Everyone who had written off Thailand had been proved wrong.

One final quality that marks the successful entrepreneur is the ability to give something back. Society is like a forest — it won't continue to flourish if we don't replenish what we take out. Too many people treat society like a slot machine: they hope to hit the jackpot while putting in as little as possible.

One of the ways I try to give something back is by giving money to various charities including the Duangprateep Foundation. The charity is based at the heart of Klong Toey, Bangkok's biggest slum area, close to the city's port. Wooden huts and makeshift houses sit atop walkways and planks only inches above the fetid water. Stroll around here when it is 40 degrees Celsius, and the stench and the heat are overwhelming. The area is home to thousands of people, a place where drug abuse is rampant, HIV infection rates are appalling, and loan sharks patrol the alleys. Some of the inhabitants are illegal squatters, so in the eyes of the government they don't officially exist.

And yet, in the middle of this nightmare, one woman has created a vision of hope. Prateep Ungsongtham was born into poverty in the slum. A determined child, she worked at a fireworks factory and a shipyard for a pittance before helping to found the first school for the children of the slum. The school became famous and attracted national attention. In 1978, she was awarded the Magsaysay Award, the Asian equivalent of the Nobel Prize, and with the US$20,000 prize money set up her own charitable foundation.

It is a moving experience to wander around the spotless classrooms full of smiling kids dressed in clean, neatly pressed uniforms. For a tiny amount of money, these children are taught to read and write and given a real chance to escape the clutches of their dreadful environment. The foundation also helps the adult community with education, legal advice, and health services. More importantly, Khun Prateep has helped to give the whole slum community hope and a measure of self-respect. One leaves the foundation feeling very humble.

We have also started a scholarship program in my father's name to provide educational support to disadvantaged children. All the proceeds I receive from this book will go to these charities.

On the subject of humility, I do not begin to presume that the 25 "rules" presented in this book are the be-all and end-all of becoming a successful entrepreneur. Rules are for the obedience of fools and the guidance of wise men. They are merely guidelines, and you can break or bend all of them and still be successful. When all is said and done, most of what I have said here is common sense. It remains only for me to wish you the very best of luck, for that is the one quality without which none of us can prosper.

Chronology

1949	William E. Heinecke born in Virginia, United States.
1952	Family moves to Tokyo, Japan.
1956	Family moves to Hong Kong.
1960	Family moves to Kuala Lumpur, Malaysia.
1963	Family moves to Bangkok, Thailand.
1965	Starts selling ads and writing for the *Bangkok World*
1967	Graduates from International School, Bangkok Founds office cleaning and radio advertising companies — Inter-Asian Enterprise and Inter-Asian Publicity.
1968	Marries Kathleen Ann Worthen.
1970	Founds Minor Holdings.
1974	Inter-Asian Publicity bought by Ogilvy & Mather.
1975	Opens Mister Donut, first international fast-food franchise outlet in Thailand. Fall of Saigon. U.S. withdraws troops from Thailand.
1976	First hotel venture: Takes over The Royal Garden Resort, Pattaya.
1978	Resigns from chairmanship of Ogilvy & Mather to devote full attention to Minor Holdings.
1979	Opens and closes Mister Donut in Malaysia.
1980	First Pizza Hut opens in Pattaya. First devaluation of the Thai baht — 20 to 23 baht to the dollar.
1983	Forfeits Railway Hotel, Hua Hin.
1984	Royal Garden Resort, Hua Hin, opens.
1986	First Swensen's ice cream parlor opens.
1988	Enters joint venture agreement with U.K. company Taylors Technical Services to provide offshore catering in the Gulf of Thailand.

Royal Garden Village, Hua Hin, opens.
Buys 25% of Saatchi & Saatchi (Thailand) Ltd.
Sells Mister Donut franchise in Thailand to Central Group.

1989   Pizza Hut home-delivery service starts.
Acushnet Foot-Joy Golf Glove factory opens.

1990   Esprit joint venture starts.

1991   Pizza plc, Minor Corporation plc and Royal Garden Resorts plc listed on Stock Exchange of Thailand.

1992   Royal Garden Riverside opens.
New Royal Garden Resort, Pattaya, opens.
Siam Par joint venture initiated to represent Lancôme cosmetics and perfume brands.
First Sizzler restaurant opens.

1993   Factory to supply cheese to pizza restaurants opens.
Ice cream factory opens to supply Swensen's.

1994   Royal Garden Riverside Hotel becomes Marriott.
Hundredth restaurant opens under The Pizza Company.
Launch of Red Earth Cosmetics.

1995   Regent Chiangmai Resort Hotel opens.
Royal Garden Resort Plaza, Pattaya, opens.
One-telephone-number pizza home delivery introduced.
Piper Aircraft and Sheaffer exclusive distribution contract signed.
Ripley's Museum, Pattaya, opens.

1996   First Dairy Queen opens.
Boots U.K. joint venture.

1997   Ripley's Museum, Hong Kong, opens.
Asian crisis starts in July. Baht begins floating.
Boots retail joint venture company is sold.
Givaudan-Roure joint venture company is sold.

1998   First hotel in Vietnam opens in Haiphong.
Sale of Siam Par joint venture company (exclusive distribution of Lancôme cosmetics).

Purchases 25% of Regent Hotel, Bangkok.

Two-hundredth restaurant opens under The Pizza Public Company.

1999   Sells Acushnet Foot-Joy Golf Glove joint venture factory.

Hostile takeover of Regent Bangkok initiated by Goldman Sachs.

Launches joint venture with Mandara Spa for Thailand.

Launch of Chicken Treat and Burger King.

2000   Lawsuit with Tricon over Pizza Hut Thailand.

Dairy Queen celebrates one hundredth outlet.

2001   Launch of The Pizza Company.

Joint agreement signed with Societe Bic.

Launch of Bossini.

Launch of Bloom cosmetics.

Opening of JW Marriott Phuket Resort and Spa.

Sells 25% shareholding in Saatchi & Saatchi (Thailand).

Rebranding of Bangkok Marriott Riverside Hotel to "Bangkok Marriott Resort and Spa".

Rebranding of Royal Garden Resort Pattaya to "Pattaya Marriott Resort and Spa".

Rebranding of Royal Garden Resort Hua Hin to "Hua Hin Marriott Resort and Spa".

Rebranding of Royal Garden Village to "Anantara Resort and Spa Hua Hin".

September 11 World Trade Center disaster in New York.

2002   Appointment as Cessna Aircraft Company exclusive representation for Thailand.

Opening of Marriott Vacation Time Share, Phuket.

Acquisition of Le Meridien Baan Boran Hotel, Chiang Rai.

RGR receives A− credit rating.

The **MINOR** Group

Food Retailing and Manufacturing

Hotel, Entertainment and Property Development

Marketing and Retailing

Bibliography

Ericksen, Gregory, *What's Luck Got To Do With It?* (John Wiley & Sons, New York, 1997).

Krass, Peter (ed.), *The Book of Business Wisdom* (John Wiley & Sons, New York, 1997).

Krass, Peter (ed.), *The Book of Leadership Wisdom* (John Wiley & Sons, New York, 1998).

Lowe, Janet, *Bill Gates Speaks* (John Wiley & Sons, New York, 1998).

Marriott, J.W., *The Spirit to Serve, Marriott's Way* (HarperBusiness, New York, 1997).

The Performance Group, *The Keys to Breakthrough Performances* (Bjelland, Dahl & Partners, Oslo).

Randall, Charles, *The Folklore of Management* (John Wiley & Sons, New York, 1997).

Spendolini, Michael J., *The Benchmarking Book* (American Management Association, New York, 1992).

Index